Get Your Ship Together!

Charting A Course To True Wealth

Del Lewis

Deep
Pacific
Press

ISBN: 978-1-64184-190-0 (Paperback)
978-1-64184-191-7 (ebook)

Deep Pacific Press
117 E. 37th Street
#580
Loveland, CO 80538
www.DeepPacificPress.com

CONTENTS

To three incredible women in my life – my forever young mother, Gayle Lewis, who inspired and encouraged me with her literary passion and genius, my beautiful wife, Jackie Lewis, who lifts me up and supports me in countless ways, and to my amazing and beautiful daughter, Claire Lewis, whose passion for reading and creativity with the written word has propelled me though this amazing book writing voyage!

FORWARD

Let's face it, if you grew up with an older brother and he also happened to be the oldest sibling in the family, you probably know, like I painfully do, that he swore, from the moment you entered into this world, that you would forever be his slave.

I actually have two older brothers but I am specifically talking about the oldest in the family. He also happens to be the author of this book, and even today, despite the fact that "we're all grown up" with families of our own, he didn't really *ask* me if I would write this foreword, but rather "my loving older brother" suggested it was my duty to do so. Some things never change.

Truth be told, I have been totally blessed to have endured the beatings, weggies, slap fights, and occasional hours-long bathroom lock-ups simply because all those things made me stronger - in a warped "little brother" sort of way. Believe it or not, I felt actually loved through it all.

When I was about twenty years old, my brother Del was starting businesses, making moves, and accomplishing more before the age of twenty-five than most people are accomplishing by age forty. To say I was a bit envious would be an understatement.

So what is a younger brother to do? Simple, ask him to partner with you in building a business of course; and that is exactly what I did. And to my surprise he agreed. So off we went. We bought, re-designed, and ran a fine dining restaurant in the heart of Washington, DC.

For Del, it was another adventure to hone his business and entrepreneurial skills and continue to challenge himself. For me, it was an opportunity to tap into the mind of an organized and disciplined brother who could keep me from falling off the rails.

After many months of planning, dealing with accountants, lawyers, food purveyors, hiring and firing staff, and dealing with the fickleness of your typical restaurant patron, we did our best to stay afloat, but unfortunately we had to let the dream go.

When we finally locked the doors for good I felt as though something had died inside of me. Here I was a trained and accomplished chef who had just failed at his first business attempt. But I noticed a completely different take on the situation from my brother. Del immediately calculated the closing from a purely business mindset rather than the wildly emotional mindset I was beholding.

When I asked him several weeks after we closed why he seemed so calm, his answer was quick and direct. "We were under-capitalized from the beginning which greatly reduced our ability to ride out the typical ups and downs of the restaurant business. Our working capital as a percentage of operating cost was at least 30% below average.

Furthermore he said, "after careful review of the past 6 months of our operation, it also seems evident that daily amounts of Cash were being skimmed by high level employees from our daily sales". His poise in the moment was completely awe inspiring.

Even though I had no clue what he was talking about – working capital and industry averages, I did feel a sense of relief in at least having some answers. But unfortunately that didn't stop me from a downward spiral into depression and guilt.

About six months after we closed the restaurant I ran into Del at a function of friends and family. He quickly noticed my glazed eyes and that unique look that says "I am a loser for life". Even in my funk I could tell my overall demeanor worried him.

He pulled me aside and asked one simple question…

"What the Fuck are you doing with your life?"

And before I could even begin to respond, he went into full-on "older brother mode". It seemed like a flashback to twenty years ago. He looked me straight in the eyes and said, stop blaming yourself for what happened, stop acting as if you have no talent and won't amount to anything and for God's sake, "GET YOUR SHIT TOGETHER"

Boom! That's when it happened. In that five minute lashing I was shaken back to reality and I realized I had to stop feeling sorry for myself. In that moment I was reminded I had a brother who deeply cared for and loved me. His ways might have been stern and at times painful, but he was always very effective at getting his message across.

Several years later I got a call from my other older brother. He and I are only one year and 10 days apart in age. We were inseparable growing up and we remain close to this day.

On this particular day he was calling to tell me how he was feeling down because his business – a cabling company

- was failing and he also suspected some foul play from his business partner. He told me he was most likely going to have shut his business down. I could definitely feel his pain. It was like déjà vu all over again.

I tried my best to console him and lift his spirits but could feel I wasn't making much of an impact. I think we were just too close, and too much alike.

And then it hit me, I said "hey, have you called Del?" I said, I think it may be time for you to get introduced to his "GET YOUR SHIT TOGETHER" conversation.

Long story short, he did, and went on to do some incredible things with his life.

My oldest brother, Del, is truly a genius when it comes to figuring out the building blocks necessary to achieve success. Over the years he has not only created for himself many incredible outcomes, but he has introduced me, and countless others, to a new and unique way to look at, and build, wealth.

Maybe it's time you and he had that "special" conversation!

To your success!
Brian Lewis
Chef, Entrepreneur, Author, and "Little Brother"

1

A Distant Ship's Smoke
On The Horizon

There's really nothing worse than sitting at a desk, in a small unassuming office, staring out a window with the view of a parking lot, listening to your co-workers bitch about meaningless trivialities because the work at hand is so boring that there's nothing better to do.

And that was exactly the situation I found myself in the day I received The Call.

I call it The Call because, at least to me, it holds the same significance as The Catch. Now if you're not familiar with, or don't give any deference to, The Catch, then you're either under 50, a Dallas Cowboy fan, or not a professional football fan at all, or (god forbid), all three!

Actually, if you're under 50 that's okay; I was there once, so I won't hold that against you. But being guilty of the other two is practically a mortal sin! Just kidding. (Sort of).

Okay, for those of you who don't know, and are dying to know the significance of The Catch, let me just say it was a touchdown pass from the San Francisco 49ers Joe Montana (one of the greatest quarterbacks to ever play the game) to Dwight Clark. The Catch sealed the victory in the 1981 National Football League NFC Championship game against the Dallas Cowboys, and arguably was the start of the San Francisco 49ers dynasty in the 1980s. Now even though I'm a diehard Washington Redskins fan, I'm a football fan first and foremost and can appreciate the importance of The Catch to NFL legend and history.

Similarly, for me, The Call was much like a perfectly thrown spiral touchdown pass, but in the form of a personal, and business, connection and the start of a business journey, or voyage. The quarterback in this case was a highly successful entrepreneur and the recipient, much like Dwight Clark, was a relatively unknown (until then) young professional – Me.

While The Call might have been the start of it all, the story certainly doesn't begin there.

So where should I start? The beginning always seems like a logical place, but that's so damn boring, so let's start somewhere in the middle and see where that leads us.

2

Stop The Ship I Wanna Get Off!

It's 3 a.m. at the bar, and it's just me and the bartender. As he comes to the end of his rant, he pours me another drink. At that moment I begin to cry!

Now, I'm not the crying type. I can probably count on one finger the number of times I'd cried as an adult up to that point in my life. But at that moment I had reached the end of my rope!

As I struggle to lift my head off the bar, I take in my surroundings through glazed eyes. The bar is a tastefully appointed, solid wood, crescent-shaped structure with ample room for at least 12 bar stools, and each stool, like the one my butt is resting on, is a cushy arm chair perched four and a half feet off the ground.

Through the reflection in the full-length mirror that runs the length of the bar I can see several tables and chairs that make up the bar lounge area. All, of course, are completely empty now because last call was a few hours ago.

Adjacent to the bar area is the downstairs dining room. Six tables with comfortable seating for at least 30 people, each with a brand new lily-white table cloth, and perfectly set with silver and glassware for tomorrow's lunch crowd.

My mind wanders up the carpeted flight of stairs to the upper dining room where I know from memory, and careful calculation, that anywhere from 68 to 74 people can enjoy a dining and entertainment experience like none other in our nation's capital.

As I reminisce, and take this all in with a throbbing head, puffy, watery eyes, and the embarrassment that only a self-proclaimed stoic can feel as he blubbers uncontrollably, it finally sinks in that this just might be the last time I'll see this place. And at that moment, that was more than I could handle! Hence the torrent of tears.

You see, the bartender, who was more than twice my age, and who had just finished berating me, actually worked for me!

Although I was only 25, I owned the bar, the restaurant, all the tables and chairs, the tablecloths, silverware, all the liquor behind the bar, the food in the walk-in refrigerators, and all the wine in the cellar.

And this guy, who thought he was god's gift to the beverage industry had just finished telling me how stupid

I was and how bad a restaurateur I was. And the reason I broke down crying was because at that moment I figured he was probably right.

About a year before this tear-filled night, my younger brother Brian and I had raised money and bought this bar and restaurant. Brian was, and still is, an ultra-talented chef, trained in the states and Europe. He had found an opportunity to purchase an out-of-business Mexican restaurant that was being foreclosed on by the bank.

Brian had assembled a team of restaurant managers, kitchen personnel, and wait staff, and he had recruited our good friend John Douglas, a Marine Corps helicopter pilot, who was also a magician with a hammer and a saw. Together we transformed a defunct casual Mexican restaurant into one of the up-and-coming places to see, and to be seen, in Washington, D.C.

Because this was Brian's grand idea, and because he had found the deal, we named the place after him. As a kid his nickname was Beezer, and that just seemed to fit – BEEZER'S.

The mayor of D.C. attended our grand opening, and our special guest of honor was Ms. Dionne Warwick, a mega pop star at the time. She is second only to Aretha Franklin as the most-charted female vocalist of all time.

5

Our restaurant was located in an ideal area in northwest Washington, nestled between Georgetown and the White House. The area was a combination of high-end apartments, condos, hotels, and the plush offices of high-powered lawyers and lobbyists. These folks loved to drink, and they had their favorite bartenders whom they would follow from job to job and bar to bar.

Somehow, two of the area's "rock star" bartenders ended up working for us. Their names were Paul and Milton. Milton had spent several years tending bar at The Capital Hilton, one of D.C.'s finest hotels. He was affectionally known to his "followers" as "Milton From The Hilton." The other guy's name was Paul. Before gracing us with his presence Paul had worked for years at The Prime Rib, an upscale restaurant and bar that catered to the Washington business elite. It was Paul who I had the "pleasure" of listening to, and drinking with, that fateful night.

In addition to outstanding food, we had great entertainment, and on the weekends the house was usually packed. And our bar was always three-deep Thursday through Saturday. In the interest of full disclosure, I have to admit that one of the major reasons our bar was packed most every afternoon and evening was because of the jerk now standing before me, verbally pelting me with insults. But, we were making serious money!

And simultaneously going broke.

So, there I was, sitting in a puddle of my own tears, visually summing up my surroundings, and convinced I was looking at both the biggest success AND biggest failure of my 25-year-old life.!

I pulled myself off the bar stool, wiped my eyes, blew my nose and shouted, "ENOUGH IS ENOUGH!" I regained some of my mojo and told Paul "to shut the hell up." I finished my drink, ordered Paul to leave everything as it was. We'd clean up tomorrow. I called a cab, dropped him off at his place, then headed home myself. Yes, I was so pathetic that night that I even gave that bastard a ride home!

I was back at the restaurant around 9 the following morning (technically later that same morning) but I didn't go there to finish cleaning up or to get the place ready for opening at 11 a.m., our usual time. No, I went there to slap a "Temporarily Closed" sign on the front door.

Just six hours before, at 3 a.m., when I had shouted "ENOUGH IS ENOUGH," I had meant it. I was through! At least through with the restaurant business.

At the ripe old age of 25 I had learned something very important about myself. I knew I wanted to make lots of money. I wanted wealth, fame, and fortune, and all the material trappings so often associated with wealth, fame, and fortune. And I had always thought I would do anything legal, ethical, and moral in my pursuit of money. But through this experience I had found out, very clearly, that I wouldn't do just anything for money.

I figured out that passion, and doing what I enjoy, and with the types of people I enjoy being around, is the only way for me to do it.

So, at 9 a.m., just six hours after bawling my eyes out and reveling in my own private pity party, I strode confidently up to my restaurant/bar establishment and slapped that CLOSED sign on the door! I had decided it was time to get my life back on track.

So, what did I do next?

Well, to fully understand what happened next, we need to go back a few years. Actually, we need to go back like 500 years! We need to go back to what many consider to be the heyday of wealth exploration.

Here's a little ditty to start you off...

My Version Of The Famous Kid's Poem

In fourteen hundred ninety-two
Columbus sailed the ocean blue.

He had three ships and left from Spain
He sailed through sunshine, wind, and rain.

He sailed by night; he sailed by day;
He used the stars to find his way.

A compass also helped him know
How to find the way to go.

Ninety sailors were on board;
Some men worked while others snored.

Sails full of wind, the only sound
Each man praying the earth was round.

For if it were flat, as most men thought
This expensive voyage would be for naught.

But King Ferdie, Queen Izzy, and Chris had a dream,
So, they worked together as a team.

They hoped and dreamed that in India they would arrive,
To make Spain rich, help it to prosper, and to thrive.

But instead it was America where they hit land,
And history would argue this discovery was even more grand.

So, what's the moral of my version of this sonnet?
A thought is not a thing until you put some action on it.

Back in the 15th century, everyone thought the world was flat. Then this Italian dude, backed by a Spanish couple, hops in a boat and sets sail. He's banking that there is a quicker way to get to the "Promised Land" of his day.

So he heads out of port and takes a right, instead of a left. He's not convinced the earth is flat, so he decides to push the envelope.

Long story short ....

The dude not only doesn't fall off the edge of the supposedly flat earth, but he finds a whole "new world," where the people look different, talk differently, and probably even smell different.

But Columbus is okay with all that, because he knows he can convert them to his way of thinking and get them to do his dirty work, and they have a lot of great foods, spices, and gold!

Today we think back on Columbus and wonder how he could have been so naive. You might wonder too:

- How did they not know the earth was round?
- Didn't they see the pictures taken by the astronauts from outer space?

- Why didn't they just go on the internet and check it out before they left? That certainly could have saved the crew a lot of needless worry!

- Or better yet, if they wanted certain spices and gold, why not just go online to Amazon? This stuff probably would have even qualified for Prime Shipping!

Oh no, wait a minute! Back in the 15th century they didn't have all that stuff. They were just a bunch of guys with an idea, an inkling, of how the world could be.

And they went for it!

And I'll bet you're glad they did, because today, nearly 500 years later, our lives are the way they are in large part because guys like Columbus thought there could be another way to see things.

Columbus didn't just THINK about the New World – he WENT there!

Those who don't just think, but also do, are the ones who are Truly Rich!

These are what I call The 360° Wealthy! They could also be called the True

Rich because they are Truly Rich in every sense!

Way back in the last century (i.e. the 20th), almost 500 years after Columbus set sail, got lost, and eventually discovered the New World, another young man started a journey of his own. No, he didn't find any new real estate, enslave a native population, or plunder for gold and spices. But he did get lost for a short period of time, and then eventually discover a New World; one inhabited by the 360° Wealthy.

This 20th century explorer figured out the biggest difference the between the 360° Wealthy and everybody else is that the 360° Wealthy actually do something with their wild and crazy thoughts. You see, lots of people think about lots of stuff, all the time.

But the 360° Wealthy, like maritime explorers of old, take action.

This 20th century explorer, like Columbus, found out things don't always turn out the way you plan, and also learned that wealth is multi-faceted and if you want to be really rich you need to take a 360° approach.

This is the story of a journey, of treasures found, and how to get your ship together and stop merely thinking about getting rich and actually became Truly Rich.

Ready to set sail toward your wealth?

Well turn the page!

3

Oh Ship!

Since you're so smart, I'm sure by now you've noticed my clever use of the word "ship." No, I'm not afraid to use the word "shit." In fact, it's been a major part of my lexicon for a large portion of my life (Much to the disappointment of my mother, I'm sure!)

I talk about ships because the design, building, ownership, and operation of ships, and in fact the entire maritime industry, is a wonderful metaphor for becoming part of the 360° Wealthy. Because if you understand the things it takes to "get a ship together," and make it work for you, you will understand what it takes to "get your shit together" and become a part of the 360° Wealthy, thus creating (for yourself) success, fame, fortune, freedom, fun (any and/or all of the above), however you choose to define it.

Ultimately, I define being Rich as having a life that lights you up – every day, all the time. A life that has all the stuff you want in it, in it! And, hint, hint, it's not necessarily all about money!

Let's expand a little further on the maritime analogy. A commercial ship has three main departments – the Deck department, the Engine Department, and the Steward's Department. All three of these shipboard departments work together to make a ship run efficiently and safely. Likewise, 360° Wealth is comprised of three main areas of our lives – Time, Money, and Health. When you have all three of these in abundance (however YOU define abundance) you are wealthy in a 360° way.

Taking the analogy one step further, each of our shipboard departments consists of people whose job requires them to interact with other people in each of the other departments. The Deck Department can't navigate the ship toward its destination if the Engine Department doesn't provide the power to propel the ship, and everyone in both the Deck and Engine departments would starve if the Steward's Department didn't provide the meals. Likewise, each of the three major areas of 360° Wealth (Time, Money, & Health) all have supporting areas that work together and help make 360° Wealth even better. The chief 360° Wealth supporters are Imagination, Relationships, and Things. These three run through every aspect of each main 360° Wealth area. Here's a simple example of how they could combine: (1) how you think about, or imagine, your time; (2) your relationship to your time; or (3) the things you use during certain times. The 3 major areas and the 3 supporting areas combine in various, and numerous, ways as you pursue your quest for 360° Wealth. Get the picture?

Perhaps this image will help.

Motivational speaker and coach, Tony Robbins, likes to say, "Success leaves clues." A lot happens when you're in action, and unless we take time to stop and think about some of the clues left by our actions – our successes, and especially our failures -- we're missing the boat (pun intended).

So, dive into what you see and read here. And make sure you read between the lines, because there are a lot of clues there, too. Never stop absorbing and learning. Hell, I'm still on my journey. My world is constantly evolving, and constantly getting better, more fun, and more abundant each day. I have 360° Wealth and you can, and should, too!

360° Wealth is like sailing on ALL the "seven seas," not just one. I use the term "seven seas" just like the rest of the nautical world does -- as a figure of speech to capture the vastness of the world's bodies of waters. The seven seas of the 360° Wealthy is also a figure of speech, one I use to capture the many and varied ways to get, and be, Rich.

Over the centuries, the phrase "the seven seas" has been used to refer to different bodies of water at various times and places. The ancient Romans called the lagoons separated from the open sea near Venice the "septem maria" or seven seas. Just in case you were wondering, most current sources state the "seven seas" as Atlantic, Pacific, Arctic, and Indian Oceans, as well as the Mediterranean Sea, the Caribbean Sea, and the Gulf of Mexico.

We're going to be exploring a lot here, and before we're done I'm going to share with you the seven keys to "having it all," each of which when tied together will propel you toward wealth in ALL its glory. When you understand and use this simple yet uber-powerful tool you can become one of the 360° Wealthy.

Here's a little teaser ....

4

ACTA NON VERBA!

Acta Non Verba is Latin for "Deeds Not Words." It's the motto of the college I graduated from, and is pretty much the polar opposite of doing nothing!

So, you can imagine what a stretch it was for me to do nothing immediately after shutting down my restaurant. But I needed to chill, to regroup, and to figure out my next steps.

For roughly five years before I posted the "Temporarily Closed" sign on our restaurant door I had been going non-stop. After graduating college, I had been sailing the proverbial Seven Seas as a marine engineer aboard various commercial ships, I had been investing in and managing real estate, and in my free time I'd been traveling the world playing my version of the role of International Bachelor.

So there I was, 25 years old and "self un-employed!"

I had just legislated myself out of a job by posting that sign on my restaurant door. On the one hand I was relieved that I didn't have to deal with the crap of running a fine-dining restaurant in the heart of a major city, but on the other hand I had no idea what I was going to do.

Yes, the result was I did nothing, but it's more accurate to say I was paralyzed.

Days went by, the restaurant remained closed, and I gradually realized that I was never going to open those doors again!

At first I moved at a snail's pace, seemingly just going through the motions of formally shutting the business down. I had the hard conversation with the bank, hired a forensic accountant to close the books and hopefully figure out where all the cash had disappeared to. I was pretty sure our cracker-jack manager, Don; and my rock-star bartenders had a pretty good idea where the money was. I had the conversation with my brother, Brian, which was easier than I thought because he was feeling the crushing weight of the business as well.

After all the administrative and fiduciary responsibilities were tidied up, I began to figure out my next move. I'd been bitten by the entrepreneurial bug so I knew I would go back into business for myself but I just wasn't sure what I could do. I kept asking myself, "What can I do next?"

Which, of course, is absolutely the wrong question!

There's a saying among sailors – "Any port in a storm." This is great seafaring advice if the shit's hit the fan and you're in the middle of it all. When that happens, it makes total sense to get into the calm, and ideally safer water of a port; any port.

But after you've weathered the storm and the shit's already hit the fan, and you're now assessing the damage, counting the bodies and you've got some time to think, you don't need to settle for just any port.

For me, at that particular time, asking the question "what CAN I do next?" was just like settling for the next available port.

Thank God, when I asked "what can I do" all the answers I got sucked! Because if I had sailed into the next "safe" port, or settled for what was easiest to do, or what I could do, I never would have gotten The Call.

After you've weathered the storm (which I had) and you've got some time to think (which I did), the right question to ask is "What do I WANT to do next?"

This is an infinitely more powerful question, and the answers you will discover when you ask this question will simply amaze you.

Oh, and at the risk of stating the obvious, the real power of this question comes when you don't put any restrictions on what you want or any thoughts about why what you want can't happen. For example, if you say "I want to be president of the United States" but then you follow that up by saying, "But that's really hard to do, I need campaign money, a strong team, name recognition, political support, etc., etc." then, to use a good shipboard term – you're dead in the water!

Ask yourself the question, give yourself the answer, or answers, then take action! Do that, and the rest is, as they say, "history."

Speaking of history, the quest for maritime dominance on the Atlantic Ocean holds a ton of 360° Wealthy Clues. Let's see which ones pop out for you ....

"Chief, give her all you've got!"

The Blue Riband of The Atlantic was a prize awarded to the ship that made the fastest Atlantic crossing. Because of all the different ways to navigate from Point A to Point B, the award was not given based on actual miles travelled, but rather on the top speed a ship achieved between two specific points along the route.

The prevailing winds and currents made the westbound crossing, from Europe to America, more difficult than the eastbound, so the Blue Riband was divided into two prizes, one for each direction. The westbound crossing, because it was more difficult, was viewed as more prestigious.

The race for the prize would begin when a ship left its last port of call and was making full cruising speed. Westbound this was usually off the southwest tip of England. The clock would stop when the ship arrived at the mouth of New York Harbor.

What started out as a way to attract more business -- speed being the key -- turned into an all-out obsession. Shipping companies, naval architects, marine engineers, and even entire national governments were consumed by the need for speed, and the prize.

As you get your ship together, and begin to build 360° wealth, it's super important to keep in mind what you want.

Sure, you might want to make a lot of money, or perhaps you may have a civic or social passion, like saving the world. A major key to "your success" is understanding "your quest."

What's going to propel your ship forward? In the late 1800's and 1900's it was commercial pre-eminence at sea, and the Blue Riband was the primary indicator of that.

You are unique; your desires, wants, aspirations, gifts, talents, and resources are unique and different from anybody else's.

In the early 1800's the introduction of the steam engine propelled the industry and its respective businesses forward (pun intended!). In 1807, Robert Fulton, considered the Father of the Modern Steam Engine, launched The Claremont, a steamboat that cut the travel time from New York City to Albany, NY, from three days down to thirty-two hours. Twelve years later, a group of businessmen from Savannah, Georgia, invested in, built, and successfully sailed a small steamship across the Atlantic. Game on!

It's interesting to note that because the United States was, and still is, so rich in natural resources, most U.S. business people in the 1800's were primarily occupied with swiftly moving cargo around the United States. Most foreign cargo still went under sail. It wasn't until the early 1900's that the steam craze hit U.S. international shipping.

It was a different story for the British, though. The great wealth of the British Empire was tied primarily to the overseas wealth generated by its colonies. For the British government, steam was absolutely the way to go.

Great Britain not only needed to get bulk cargo like metals, grains, and finished goods from their colonies back to England, but there was also great demand to shuttle passengers to the United States and Canada. And the other cargo that was so vital to the growth and efficiency of any large industrialized country, and certainly Great Britain, was mail.

Yes, back then they actually wrote letters, and much of the business of the day was conducted via mail. There was no air mail, of course, so it all travelled on ships. In fact, anything that had to move between the continents had to move by ship.

I've always found it curious that mail, yes simple letters and packages, was the impetus for the creation of a massive industry -- the maritime industry.

It takes a ton of money to build a ship, and I'm sure you feel like it takes a ton of money to live your life the way you want to live it. And you're right, one of the fuels of the 360° Wealthy certainly is money. (But it's not the only fuel.)

And who has most of the money? Governments! Most governments have more money than individuals. So it was up to governments to finance the building and operation of ships. We already saw this to be the case with our buddy Chris (Columbus that is, in case you forgot). The Nina, Pinta, and Santa Maria were built and run on Spanish government money.

Well, it was no different in the late 1800's and all though the 20th century. Governments had to come up with the lion's share of the cash to build and grow their maritime industries. And mail -- the effective delivery of mail -- became the rallying call for government support.

By the way, here's a clue: Money follows value!

And if you can find the deepest pockets with the most money, and figure out how to add value for them, they will give you their money.

Simply put, people and entities with lots of money will gladly give it to you if you solve their problems.

So, in the latter part of the 19th and 20th centuries, maritime entrepreneurs in Great Britain were building steamships like crazy with government subsidies because the British government wanted the mail delivered!

Now as you can imagine, the British government, just like the rest of us, wanted mail delivered on a regular basis. This meant that ships built with British government money had to sail on regular schedules, and travel on set routes, from Point A to Point B to Point C.

Believe it or not, this was a whole new concept for the marine trade. Before that, most ships were what we call today "Tramps," a ship that went wherever it could to pick up and deliver cargo. For example, if a company in Barcelona had cargo it needed to get to London it would charter (that's the fancy maritime term for "hire" or "rent") a ship. The ship would go from Barcelona to London, offload its cargo, then look for another cargo to take from London to anywhere. Tramp ships and their crews would often stay at sea for years until they got a cargo heading back to their home port.

Obviously, this system of tramping around the world wouldn't work for regular mail delivery. And, in addition to mail, a different type of cargo was becoming even more lucrative -- people!

No, I'm not talking about that 15th century people-hauling business, more commonly known as slavery. No, in the late 1800's, and first half of the 1900's, there were a whole bunch of people who actually wanted to be transported somewhere else. And they were willing to pay for it.

As the age of steam propulsion grew, the travel time between the continents dramatically dropped, and people, especially from Europe, were flocking to the United States.

But it was mail that "paid the freight." Governments around the world were providing huge subsidies to shipping companies if they would carry the country's mail over regularly timed sea routes. These shipping companies became known as "Liners" because they (more or less) travelled in a straight line between Point A and Point B. During this period, Great Britain led the way, granting subsidies and building steamships.

The heated competition between Great Britain, Germany, and eventually France, during the late 19th century, led to vast technical advances and bigger and faster ships. Progress was astounding. Liners grew from 3,000 gross tons to 10,000. Ships doubled in length from 300 to nearly 600 feet.

In the mid-to-late 1800's, Cunard Line, the parent company of today's well-known passenger ship, the Queen Elizabeth II (QE2), was the 800-pound gorilla of the day.

After decades of Cunard supremacy on the North Atlantic, the U.S. Congress awarded an American businessman,

Edward Knight Collins, a mail subsidy of $385,000 a year. That's the equivalent to over $7.5 million today.

Collins built three luxurious ships and captured the Blue Riband speed record, averaging a speed of over thirteen knots, and making the cross-Atlantic voyage more than seven hours faster than the fastest Cunard ship. But Collins' success was short lived. After two of his ships sank, drowning hundreds of passengers, Congress pulled his subsidies, and he lost his company.

So, let's think about you getting rich in light of what we're seeing in the shipping industry in the late 1800's and early 1900's.

For the shipping entrepreneurs of that day, speed was key! And the ability to deliver cargo (people, goods, and mail) to set destinations, at set times, was also a measure of success. It took lots of money, and there was a fair amount of risk in delivering the product and service.

On the flip side, demand for a shipping company's service was growing. Why? Because there was a value to the offer. People wanted to get places that they couldn't get to before -- at least not easily.

What's happening in your world? What are the areas of value in your sphere of influence?

Back then, it was ship speed and voyage duration.

But now, what actions can you take to add value? How can you solve the problems of others?

You need to take all these factors into account as you get your ship together and begin to navigate your Seven Seas of Success.

Here's another "New World" concept for you to consider as you set sail.

The key to your success and your ability to join the ranks of the 360° Wealthy is not always about building a better ship, but about building a more unique ship.

In other words, to use a couple of clichés, the True Rich don't always look to "replace the wheel" with something completely new, but rather most of the time huge success is found when you figure out how to "build a better mousetrap." The course to success often involves uniqueness, and slight variations in things we already have available.

And it all starts with a better question: What do I want?

Sometimes, however, asking yourself a great question doesn't always produce a great answer. All I can say is keep asking.

That's what I did, and the answer kind of surprised me!

5

"You Want To Do What???"

There is something about self-inflected exhaustion that makes one see the truth. I can't tell you what it is, why it is, or how it works, but for me it certainly does. Something just hit me somewhere between mile three and mile four on my run one day, and I realized, I wanted to own and operate ships!

In the months since I had temporarily (aka permanently) closed my restaurant I had been working out like a man possessed. Every day I either ran four to five miles, swam 20-30 laps in an Olympic sized pool, lifted weights, or played racquetball; and some days I did them all. I didn't have any money but I had a hell of a lot of time on my hands. And all during that time I kept asking myself the question, "What do you want to do?" Before that day I didn't get any clear answers but one day, for some reason, it all became crystal clear. And when I say crystal clear, I mean I saw the whole picture. I saw exactly what it would look like in super great detail.

I now knew exactly what I wanted. I wanted to start a shipping company, build new ships and buy existing ships, then own and operate them around the world for great profit. Simple, right?

Here I was, essentially a kid, with no money, looking to break into an industry dominated by old white men; most of whom nowadays aren't even American, and I wanted to set it all up in a very specific way (more on that a little later).

I remember telling one of my childhood buddies and best friend about my next career move and he gave me a look like I had two heads and asked, "Where did you get such a crazy idea?"

I looked him straight in the eye and said "Francis Gibbs."

Francis Gibbs was not your stereotypic entrepreneur. Although a brilliant marine engineer and naval architect, he had no formal training in either of these two disciplines. Francis dreamed of designing and building the world's safest and fastest ship for almost 40 years before he was able to manifest it. Because of childhood sicknesses, he didn't graduate from high school until he was 20. He entered Harvard as a freshman, only to drop out and return home a year later, so he could cross the Atlantic on a steamship and learn more about ship design, construction, and operation.

Francis scrimped and saved enough money to book passage on the Cunard Line passenger ship, Mauretania. The ship set sail on November 16, 1907, and it was a typical winter Atlantic crossing, with high winds and high seas. Francis' brother, Frederic, accompanied him, and while most passengers stayed safely tucked away in their cabins, Francis and Frederic endured the bad weather to roam all areas of the ship and take copious notes. They were particularly interested in the brand-new steam turbines that propelled the great ship.

Francis did end up going back to college. He attended Columbia, then went on to law school; both at the insistence of his father. When he graduated from law school he began practicing real-estate law – and hated every minute of it.

He hated every minute of law school, and every minute spent practicing law, and was determined to get into the shipping industry, come hell or high water! Here was a man who asked the question "What do I WANT to do," and he got a very specific answer. My hero!

He passionately taught himself the dual crafts of naval architecture and marine engineering by reading professional journals and meticulously observing, whenever he could, the largest and fastest ships of the day.

After you decide what you want, passion and persistence are essential if you want to be successful. It also really helps to love what you're doing. I think one of the biggest mistakes anyone can make is to do something because you think you should, or heaven forbid, because someone else thinks you should. When you do that you own an obligation, not a passion.

Hey, take it from someone who's done it multiple times, crossing the Atlantic (literally and metaphorically) is no easy feat, especially in winter. And believe me, your life will face some "winters." Passion and persistence will carry the day and help you get safely to port.

And so it was that on the Virginia shore on a cold, blustery day in February 1950, a giant shipyard crane gently dropped a 55-ton steel plate to the dry-dock floor of the Newport News Shipbuilding and Dry Dock Company. At that moment the foundation was being laid for what would become the fastest, safest, and most luxurious ship in the world. It would take two years and over $75 million (almost $800 million today) to build her. She would be christened The S.S. United States, and would become an American treasure and the envy of the world maritime industry.

Six short months later, just before half-past six in the morning on July 7th, 1950, all three whistles of the S.S. United States simultaneously blasted the news that the ship had shattered the eastbound speed record. The S.S. United States had captured the fabled Blue Riband, which had eluded American passenger vessels for nearly a century.

Not only was she fast and sleek but she was built for maximum safety. Her interior was completely fireproof. Except for the grand pianos in the first-class salon, and the cutting boards in the various ship's galleys (kitchens), no wood was used in any of the ship's public rooms, accommodations, or crew quarters. Even the upholstery and curtains were specially treated to be fire resistant.

As the flagship of United States Lines, the S.S. United States was the most graceful, modern, powerful, and sleek vessel in the world. With her two red, white, and blue funnels, she struck such a pose on the water and became the gold standard of maritime travel.

Francis Gibbs hadn't just thought about the fastest, safest, sleekest ship in the world; he actually built it!

Almost 20 years after the keel (aka the foundation of the ship) was first laid on the shores of Virginia, a young family of six -- mom, dad, and four boys aged 8 to 1 -- pulled their light tan Volkswagen bus through the salt-air rusted gates of the Port of La Harve in France. They drove through the throng of fork lifts, longshoremen, wires, ropes, and dockside cranes down to the cargo staging and loading area of Francis Gibbs' ship, the famed S.S. United States, affectionally known as The Big U.

The VW bus was full of suitcases, trunks, canvas bags full of toys, Kodak Instamatic cameras, and mementos of the past three years spent in Africa. The Lewis family was heading home after an adventure-filled Peace Corps assignment in East Africa and a summer vacation spent touring Europe. When the minibus they had purchased direct from the German factory and had delivered to them in Lisbon, Portugal, was stowed safely aboard the ship, they ascended the gangway and embarked on a voyage that would eventually shape one little 8-year-old's life.

The Big U was heading home too! This was to be the last leg of her final voyage. The four days we spent aboard the fastest ship in the world knifing through the summer Atlantic at unchallenged speeds was truly a thrill, and that experience instilled in me a passion for the maritime industry that would lie dormant for almost 20 years, but would be rekindled in a big way -- when I got The Call!

Francis Gibbs knew exactly what he wanted, and it totally lit him up. He spent 40 years pursuing his dream and ultimately build the greatest passenger ship of his day. At the end of that great ship's life a young man was inspired in such a way that, unbeknownst to him, he started on a journey, a voyage, that would forever shape his life and open up a new world of wealth and a new way to see how true wealth is created.

Somewhere between miles three and four on my run that day I knew I wanted to own and operate ships and I knew at that very moment it was time to get my ship together and get under way.

Ah, I think we've just constructed the first blade in our 360° Wealth propeller – AWARENESS! In other words you gotta be aware of what it is you want. And the best way to find that out? Keep asking yourself the question and don't settle for any answer that doesn't completely light you up!

Then you can begin to navigate your way toward that.

But a word of caution, my fellow shipmates: navigating toward your 360° Wealth is as much art as it is science!

Navigate to the next page and see what I mean ….

6

Charts, Courses, Rough Seas, & Desired Port Destinations

When Columbus set sail, way back when, he didn't have a cell phone or the internet. He couldn't just ask Siri how to get to America. So he navigated by the stars; actually one star in particular, the North Star. The technical term for this type of navigation is Celestial Navigation.

As you create your 360° wealth, you're going to want to know how your life is going to progress, or move, grow, and become more effective and efficient. Of course, today we have all sorts of tools, courses, resources, and help to create our wealth, but if you don't have a good grounding in the basics of how to set a course and determine if you're still on it, you'll be toast if any of your whiz-bang systems should fail or otherwise be unavailable. And along the way you're going to encounter some rough seas, so you'll need to find some Desired Port Destinations. So here's a quick "plain English" course in Celestial Navigation. This is how

Chris got to the New World., and it's a great metaphor for the basics, or foundation, of figuring out "what to do next.

Celestial navigation in a nutshell is about your physical relationship to something that's stationary. If you're able to measure your relationship to that stationary object then you can tell if you are moving in the right direction. In our lives that "stationary object" could be an income goal, a weight or physical-body goal, or a relationship or spiritual goal – it's a "stationary" target we're trying to hit. And we're constantly measuring our "physical relationship" to that target.

In our physical universe there are two primary stationary objects that we use to celestially navigate. They are the North Pole and the South Pole. Based on the way the earth spins, the North Pole and the South Pole are "stationary" as they relate to the rest of the universe (i.e. the other planets, stars, moon and sun). If we can find other objects that are close to these stationary objects we can determine if we're moving toward where we want to go, or away from where we want to go.

The North Star is the one star in the galaxy that is closest to the North Pole and because of the way the earth spins on its axis, the North Star doesn't move in relationship to the North Pole. So if you want to head in the direction of the North Pole, or anywhere in between where you currently are and the North Pole, all you have to do is measure your relationship to the North Star.

Now the North Star/North Pole relationship works great if you are sailing in the northern hemisphere, but what about down south where you can't see the North Star. Well, down there you would use the Southern Cross as your navigating object because you can't see the North Star after you go below the equator.

Let's think of the North Pole as our 360° Wealth goal, and by now you know that 360° wealth is about all the points on our ship's wheel, not just money. It's the combination of all these that we're navigating our way toward.

Okay, a little more info on celestial navigation. Hey, in addition to a unique and interesting way to look at creating true wealth, you're getting some great cocktail party conversation topics, right?

If you're heading toward the North Pole, or somewhere in that direction, all you need to do is measure how high the North Star is above the horizon. As the height of the North Star increases you know you're getting closer to the North Pole. And of course if its height is decreasing you must be travelling away from the North Pole. So, in its simplest form, celestial navigation is the measurement of the height of the North Star above the horizon. This angle is what you measure with a sextant – in degrees and minutes of arc. Obviously when the sextant tells you that the North Star is exactly overhead – a height of 90 degrees – you know you've arrived at the North Pole (latitude 90 degrees). Equally, if the height of the North Star is zero degrees – when it's touching the horizon – you know you're on the Equator (latitude 0 degrees).

This method has been used by mariners for centuries. Of course it only works in the northern hemisphere, as the North Star disappears below the horizon once the equator is crossed. So in the southern hemisphere mariners measure the height of The Southern Cross.

Now this next little tidbit will really impress your friends!

Just about everyone has heard the terms "latitude" and "longitude." but has anyone ever explained them to you in plain English? Well here goes!

The equator is what we call the middle (or center) of the earth. It's an imaginary line, like a belt that goes around the planet. It is 0 degrees latitude. Latitude lines run parallel to it and circle the earth up to the North Pole from 0 to 90 degrees for North Latitude, and latitude lines running parallel to the equator circle the earth down to the South Pole from 0 to 90 degrees for South Latitude. Vertical circles – longitude lines – run the other way (perpendicular to the equator), beginning at 0 degrees at the Greenwich Meridian running through Greenwich, England, and circling 180 degrees to east for East Longitude and 180 degrees to the west for West Longitude.

In celestial navigation, time equals distance. The cool thing is that each 15 degrees of longitude (the vertical lines) is equal to one hour (so 360 degrees equals 24 hours – one hour of the rotation of the earth corresponds to 15 degrees angle of the earth's rotation). One second of time is equal to roughly 1/4 mile at the equator.

Now you know how and why the sun comes up each day (every 24 hours). If just knowing this, and being able to bank on it each day, doesn't totally motivate you to stop just thinking about getting rich, and actually set sail toward 360° wealth, I don't know what will. (Haha) ☺

So let's come full circle (pun intended) ....

Let's think of the North Pole as the top three handles on our ship's wheel (Time, Money, and Health), and the South Pole as the bottom three handles (Imagination, Relationships, and Things). A ship is no different than a car in that you need to turn the wheel to get where you want to go. And as we turn the metaphoric ship's wheel in our model we're actually sailing the proverbial Seven Seas to create 360° Wealth. And here's the really cool thing about creating True, 360° Wealth – you get to be (in fact you have to be) in multiple parts of the world at once! Stick that in your sextant, Christopher Columbus!

Okay, now that you've got the foundation let's move out of the 15th century and back into the 21st because we need to talk about the inevitable course corrections that will be required along your voyage.

Today we have GPS in our cars and phones. And if you're like me, you can't live without it. Did you know ships have had GPS for about 40 years now? Yep, in the maritime world it's called Satellite Navigation, or SatNav for short. It was a God-send for ship's navigators because it meant they no longer had to depend strictly on human (error prone) calculations.

We all have our own personal SatNav. Ultimately, your SatNav is what keeps you out of Rough Seas and delivers you to Desired Port Destinations.

But let's get one thing straight. There is no absolute one way to get from Point A to Point B. Anytime anyone tells you that they have the absolute best (one) way to do something, you're in for Rough Seas! As you navigate your life toward 360° Wealth and your defined success you definitely want to avoid Rough Seas.

To design and build a rich life that lights you up in a 360° way, you have to look into yourself and listen to yourself. You are unique, and that's what makes you so special and ultimately will make your life so powerful. There's a way for you to do things and that's the right way for you, but it's not necessarily the only way to do it. This is your SatNav.

That being said, the various tools, tips, techniques, and strategies that you are exposed to may, or may not, be the best way for you to move forward. Ultimately, they may not be the right course for you.

But, you also must understand, and this is key:

Every time you hear about a new or different way to do things in your life, you are being offered clues that could lead you where you want, and need, your life to go.

These clues could lead you to your Ultimate Desired Port -- a life that lights you up. I can't stress enough how important it is that this has to be a life that thrills you and works the way you want it to work, which is why understanding your SatNav, and listening to it, is so important.

These clues are ultra-important for you, because they are the key to unlocking the life of your dreams. They'll direct you away from the rocky shores where your ship could run aground, and may lead you to your very own Spice Islands, where all the riches of the world await you, just as they did for Columbus.

My guess is you've been exposed to numerous writings, teachings, and trainings about how to "get rich," so what I'm offering you here might be the perfect way that resonates totally with you. Or not.

Now what do you do when the steps you're taking based on your internal SatNav don't seem to be working, or worse yet, you determine you're sailing in the wrong direction? Well my friend, at that point you course-correct!

Here's a real-world example of what I mean ....

I'd been out of college for about six months and was bored to death working at an engineering firm in Crystal City, Virginia, in the very type of 9-to-5 job I had wanted to avoid. Unfortunately, the shipping industry was in a slump at the time, so I was shoreside, twiddling my thumbs in a marine engineering job.

Now at this point in my life, early twenties, I was in pretty good shape. I looked like a typical college graduate and former athlete. But, although looking at me you might not have said I was fat, you and I would probably have agreed I could have lost a few pounds. My "workout" consisted mainly of twelve-ounce curls of Budweiser at Happy Hour!

I had a lot of time on my hands. As a result, I picked up a book called "Fit for Life" by Harvey and Marilyn Diamond. Harvey talked about losing weight and increasing our energy through what he called "Proper Food Combining." The more I read, the more I became convinced my current lifestyle was definitely Rough Sailing. I knew something had to change, and I figured I was now in possession of the complete and total answer!

My course set on my True North, and Harv and Mar had all the answers! They said that the key to a healthy, vibrant, energized body was to only eat certain foods at certain times, and to eat certain foods together. I read this about 30 years ago, so I don't recall all the particulars, but one concept I remember is only eating fruit on an empty stomach, and then waiting at least 30 minutes before eating anything else.

The rationale for this was that fruit will ferment in your stomach and become toxic unless you let it run through your body, nourish you, and then exit your stomach before eating anything else. In other words, eating fruit along with anything else would cause your stomach to become toxic, and that toxicity would sap your energy and ultimately cause you to gain weight.

I did Marilyn and Harvey's program for six or seven months and felt great. But something happened, I don't remember now exactly what, but I stopped. I went back to my old ways. But over the years, I've come to realize I still use many of their teachings in everyday life -- just not the entire program.

Does this make their program bad or wrong? No. I think what it says is that what they had to offer me was not the End-All, Be-All, but a clue. I had gotten out of my Rough Sea of an unhealthy and overweight lifestyle and moved closer to my Desired Port Destination of looking great and feeling energized.

Intuitively, I felt exercise was missing from my course, so for my next course correction I entered my running phase. I'd get up every morning, usually just before dawn, put on my running clothes and head out for a jog. I was living in the Los Angeles area at the time, in The Valley, and my system was to run along Ventura Blvd. for a certain number of blocks, turn around and head back. Each day I'd make sure that I went a few more blocks than the day before. I actually amazed myself, because by the end I'd built up my distance to ten kilometers, or 6.2 miles!

I'd get home from my run, take a quick shower, and grab a protein bar to eat as I was driving into the office. For lunch I'd have a salad or a juice smoothie, for dinner I'd try to eat something light, but I wasn't really particular about what I ate.

I remember losing weight and feeling really good, but this too came to an end. I found it harder and harder to get out and run. Then my career changed and so did my morning routine, so I stopped running altogether. My appetite changed, and it became harder to eat a protein bar for breakfast and a salad for lunch. End result -- back to my same old ways. Was running bad or wrong? No, it was simply a clue, another way out of the Rough Seas and toward my Desired Port Destination.

Then Dr. Barry Sears came into my navigational universe. Dr. Sears wrote a book called "The Zone," and once again my life took a change for the positive. Dr. Sears professed that the key to losing weight and having tremendous energy was all about the types of foods we ate. In a nutshell, optimal health and vitality came when we ate 40% protein, 40% carbohydrates, and 30% fat.

So I tried it, and man did I feel great! I changed what I bought at the store, I bought his Zone bars and drank his Zone shakes and I told all my friends about this new "End-All, Be-All" way to live. The science behind what Dr. Sears was preaching made sense to me and I felt the proof in my body. Am I an avid disciple of Dr. Sears today? No, but he did leave me with lots of clues, and hand me off to my next Course Correction.

Enter the next clue–P90x ….

I'm no different from anyone else when it comes to the persuasive effects of a good TV commercial or infomercial. So, when I happened on an infomercial of Tony Horton advertising his P90x extreme workout program I was hooked! I mean, who wouldn't be after seeing all these ripped men and women gyrating in a make-shift garage turned gym. I went online and ordered my copy of the DVD's, they arrived a few days later, and I was off to the races.

Tony's workouts were each about an hour long, and they were brutal. After each one I'd be standing in a pool of my own sweat and gasping for air. But I was hooked. I loved the way my body was starting to look, and I generally felt better.

P90x is a 13-week program, working out six or seven days a week, and I did the entire program -- TWICE! But after that I got bored. There's only so much one can take of Tony Horton (or anybody for that matter). I had gotten to the point where I knew not only his instructions verbatim, but I knew and could anticipate his various voice intonations and normal slip-ups.

So I eventually stopped working out with Tony and his gang. Is P90x the ultimate answer for me when it comes to health and fitness? Yes and no, but it definitely left clues, and was the perfect Course Correction when I needed it.

Today, I have an exercise routine and a way of eating that is a combination of a lot of programs and philosophies. What I've done is to piece together the clues and figure out a system that works for me. I feel as though I'm in a Desired Port Destination as it relates to my overall health, fitness, and nutrition.

You need to figure out two things -- what the clues are, and how you can most effectively Course Correct and use them in your life as you cruise toward 360° Wealth.

And remember, if you take these clues as 100% "gospel truth," and 100% applicable for you 100% of the time, you've fallen into a trap and could be headed for some Rough Seas.

Find the clues and avoid the traps, my friend! Ultimately, we're looking for Fair Winds and Following Seas!

There are a lot of great tools out there today to help you navigate, but if you don't know the basics you'll never understand how to best use those tools. And if you don't get the basics you won't have any idea what to do when the automated tools aren't available or, heaven forbid, they aren't working.

So let's add another blade to our 360° Wealth propeller – NAVIGATION.

Once you figure out WHAT you want, and you understand that you'll need to navigate and course-correct to get there, the next thing you gotta do is chart a course – that's "sailor-guy" talk for "you need a plan."

But how do you know what steps to take in the first place?

Simple; you don't!

And given that counter-intuitive revelation ....

I'm guessing you might want to turn the page!

7

"I Know A Guy Who Knows A Guy"

You know it's funny how certain things can happen to you seemingly out of the blue, and in hindsight, or much later, you see how profound they were. Two such things happened to me. These two incidents were years apart from each other but so profound in the cool life-altering events that followed me getting The Call, that they can't be overlooked. One had to do with the book *Atlas Shrugged* by Ayn Rand. I'll tell you about that one a little later on. The other one happened while I was sitting on the couch eating a pizza. By the way, yes, you can be in shape and still eat pizza. Isn't 360° Wealth truly awesome? More on that as well, a little later.

So, I'm on my couch getting ready to dive into my sixth slice of pizza and the character on my TV screen says something that literally spoke to me. He actually said my name! Now when a character in a movie blurts out your name, that's pretty cool, but with a last name like Lewis one might argue it's not too spectacular. The chances of hearing your name on TV are a lot greater if your name is "Lewis" than if your last name is "Muckenfuse" (this is someone's real name by the way, he's a friend of my parents). But when a character in a movie blurts out your name and uses it in a context that is in 100% alignment with what your mind has been consumed with for several months, well that's pretty amazing!

Here's the quick story ....

As I told you, at some point during my 5-mile run one typical overcast and very humid summer day in our nation's Capital I realized that what I wanted to do, without a doubt, was to own and operate ships.

That's why I was on the couch stuffing my face with pizza! (Haha).

No, seriously, I was stretched out on the couch inhaling sausage and pepperoni because I was taking a break from the frantic pace I'd been on in pursuit of my next dream. And in that moment watching a video and munching on pizza was just what the doctor had ordered.

Months before, when I had made up my mind that I was going to be a shipping tycoon (my words), I had mapped out EXACTLY how that was going to look. I knew wanted to own and operate commercial cargo ships. I knew I wanted to build a fleet of ships, and I wanted to operate them in such a way that would be a credit to the industry. Also, I was very clear about two other things – I wanted to own and operate U.S. flag ships and I wanted to have a partner to help me build this company.

The idea of building this shipping company with a partner was a super-critical part of my desire. If there was one thing I had learned from my restaurant days, it was that there was a lot about business that I didn't know. So, I had decided that I wanted to find a partner who was experienced in business, had deep pockets, and who was looking for a young energetic person who had practical maritime experience. I actually went so far in my course charting (aka imagination and planning) that I created in my mind what the ideal partner would look like.

In my mind's eye, my ideal partner was a successful entrepreneur in his 60's (yes, my vision was of a man, but I think that had more to do with what the industry looked like at the time than anything else), he had money and he knew how to get operations financed, and he had a desire to build a business in the maritime industry but he didn't have a whole lot of maritime experience; this way my practical experience would be of tremendous value to him.

The course I plotted called for he and I to either build or buy U.S. flag ships, and together with the team we assembled, we would own and operate ships, big ships!

So you can imagine my utter surprise when I hear these particular words emanate from my TV....

"Mr. Lewis and I are going to build ships together, great big ships!"

I dropped my piece of pizza (a mortal sin, by the way) scrambled for my remote, and rewound the VCR (Yes, it was a VHS tape! – one I actually had gone to the video store to pick up). I had to make sure I had heard what I thought I had heard. And, yep sure enough, that's what Ralph Bellamy's character said to Richard Gere's character in a scene in *Pretty Woman*.

The movie, if you've never seen it, is about a successful corporate raider (Edward Lewis, played by Richard Gere) who comes to Beverly Hills to close a deal. He needs an attractive female who's not interested in a long-term relationship to accompany him at various social events while he's in town and so he decides to hire a Hollywood Boulevard hooker (Vivian Ward, played by Julia Roberts).

I won't tell you the rest of the story in case you haven't seen it.

The line that blew me away comes at the very end when James Morse (played by Ralph Bellamy) announces what he and Edward Lewis intend to do.

The parallels to that one scene and what followed after I got The Call are nothing short of amazing and offer so may clues to creating and living a 360° Wealthy life.

So where were we? Oh yeah, at this point I had gone from being a 25-year-old restaurateur failure who was job-less, income-less, and feeling hope-less, to a 25-year-old "wannabe shipping magnate" who was in shape (running, swimming, and lifting weights will do that for you), full of energy and on a mission. Actually it was more powerful than that. I was on a quest!

I was on a quest to find my James Morse. I had an avatar of my ideal business partner and a way in which I wanted our business to look. Now all I needed to do was find "That Guy!"

So first I "hit the books" then I "hit the streets." I hit the books and began consuming and learning everything I could about the business of shipping. Living in Washington, DC was a great advantage because I had access to The Library of Congress. I spent hours in there, reading all sorts of books on the history of the U.S. Merchant Marine and how shipping companies are structured and how they operate.

Then I hit the streets by talking to anybody and everybody I could think of who had any connection to the maritime industry. It's actually kind of surprising how small and close-knit the maritime industry is. Through my network, and the proverbial six degrees of separation, I was able to talk to maritime lawyers, marine engineers, maritime logistics specialists, ship owners, and ship operators. And it seemed like every time I talked to someone and told them what I wanted to do, and how I wanted to do it, everyone said "There's this guy," or "I know I guy who told me about this guy!" And each time the name John Morris would surface.

Nobody knew much about this guy, John Morris. But just about everyone told me he's the guy I should be talking to. So, my quest became more focused. At this point my chart (aka my plan) was coming alive, and my course was being set. Now not only was I looking for a certain type of partner, but I had a name!

But I'm getting a little ahead of myself. I need to tell you a little more about why it was ships for me, and I think you'll begin to see how ships and the shipping industry are the perfect analogy for you as you go for 360° Wealth. That is, of course, if you want to stop JUST THINKNG about getting rich, and actually become rich all the way around.

Are you in?

Then, "climb aboard."

That's maritime speak for "turn the damn page." ☺

8

Planes, Trains, and Automobiles

I think you'll agree that the idea of owing a shipping company is not your typical childhood dream. Most kids dream about curing a major disease, becoming a sports superstar, a rock star, or becoming the President of the United States. I have to admit, even though I'd been a passenger on The Big U when I was an impressionable eight-year-old, the idea of owning and operating ships came to me much later in my life. I always find it fascinating how the choices we make on a moment-by-moment, day-by-day basis end up collectively being the path that leads us where we want to go. The other thing I find fascinating is how we are inspired, consciously and sub consciously, by the things we see, hear, feel, learn, and experience. A huge deal in the 360° Wealth realm.

So, Planes, Trains, and Automobiles!

If you recognize the movie title you might be dating yourself. For those of you too young to remember, it's a comedy starring Steve Martin and the late John Candy about a high-strung marketing executive (Martin), and a washed-up, but eternally optimistic salesman (Candy), who sells shower curtain rings, of all things. They accidentally meet and take just about every mode of transportation known to man in an attempt to get Steve Martin home to his family in time for Thanksgiving.

It's a funny movie. But don't worry if you don't remember it, or have never seen it, because I don't wanna talk about it anyway!

Now that I have your attention, what I really wanna talk about are Trains, Trucks, and Ships! And a truck driver who very successfully navigated the Seven Seas and changed the face of international maritime shipping forever.

But first let me set the stage ....

As I'm sure you've figured out by now, (probably painstakingly) from your own real-world experience, there's a little more to it than just thinking and growing rich! Hell, if it were that simple, everyone would be uber-rich, we'd have nowhere to dock our all our yachts, and a loaf of bread would cost $100 and no one would care!

Yes, everything in our world is created from thoughts, but there's a little more to it than just that. What I want to drive home at this point is that everything we experience, see, hear, and touch, first started from a thought. Another way "to think" about this concept is to insert the word "imagination" for the word "thought."

I love Albert Einstein's quote on imagination:

"Imagination is more important than knowledge. For knowledge is limited, whereas imagination embraces the entire world, stimulating progress, giving birth to evolution."

So what do trucks and trains have to do with ships? Well today, just about everything.

Malcolm McLean grew up on a farm in the small town of Maxton, North Carolina. His father was a farmer who also worked as a mail carrier to supplement the family's income. Malcolm graduated from high school in 1931 as the country was in the midst of the Great Depression. So college was not an option. Instead he got a job at a local gas station, saved his money, and eventually bought a used cargo truck for $120. At that point Malcolm McLean's ship had set sail. From then on he was under way and making way.

He started out hauling dirt, vegetables, and other things for the farmers in the area. He drove and saved, drove and saved, drove and saved, and gradually added trucks to his small fleet and drivers to man them. This, for my money (pun intended), is "Business Building Success 101," so take note.

You never really know when imagination is going to, metaphorically, knock you upside the head, and for Malcolm the year was 1937.

He was delivering some cotton bales from North Carolina to a sea port in New Jersey. Arriving at the dock in New Jersey, he was forced to wait hours to unload his truck trailer because the longshoremen couldn't unload the trucks and load the ship as fast as the trucks were arriving. Malcom marvelled at all the time and money being wasted by this process. At the time, everything was transported either in a crate or on a pallet, and each crate or pallet was taken off the truck and put into a sling, which would then lift the cargo into the hold of the ship. McLean knew there had to be a better way.

Although the first seed of imagination hit Malcolm McLean, it would be another 19 years before he turned this imagination-inspired thought into a business. But make no mistake, the entrepreneurial navigation had begun.

Now imagination of and by itself is awesome and you should never stifle the thought process, but you should also know that oftentimes it's imagination coupled with necessity, or intense desire, that is the real combination for success. It was necessity that combined with Malcolm's imagination that ultimately created this major maritime breakthrough.

By the early 1950s, Malcolm had driven and saved, driven and saved, driven and saved, and now had a fleet of 1,776 trucks and thirty-seven transport terminals along the eastern U.S. seaboard. He had built his operation into the largest trucking fleet in the South and the fifth-largest in the country.

Necessity came into the picture when states started imposing new weight restrictions and levying more and greater fees for interstate trucking. Truck trailers passing through multiple states could be fined for loads deemed to be "overweight." The trick for truckers becomes figuring out how to haul as much weight as possible without triggering additional fees.

McLean knew there must be a more efficient way to transport cargo, and his thoughts returned to the "coastwise" ships that ran up and down the U.S. coastline. A "coastwise" ship, by the way, is just the maritime term given to a ship that calls on U.S. ports only. Coastwise ships never go foreign.

McLean envisioned that shipboard transportation could be way more cost effective than land transportation. His imaginative genius led him to envision a system where just a container, not the cargo bed chassis or the wheels, could be lifted off a truck and set on a ship. Genius!

Now here is how an "entrepreneurial navigation rock star" really makes way ....

When their imagination kicks in and they take inspired action, they take that idea and build an entire business system around it. And Malcolm McLean proceeded to do just that.

He realized that transporting "containerized cargo" was the perfect cost-effective extension of his business. Initially he figured his trucking fleet would be the centrepiece of the overall transportation network, and instead of trucks traipsing up and down the eastern coastline, he could have trucking hubs in the destination endpoints in the North and South. The ships would handle most of the transit and he'd save a ton on interstate transit fees.

As his thoughts solidified in his mind, McLean redesigned his truck trailers into two parts — a truck bed on wheels and an independent box, or container, that would be secured on top. His vision was for several stackable containers to be loaded on deck and into the hull of the ship.

He designed, and had made, shipping containers constructed of heavy steel so they could withstand rough seas and protect their contents. They were designed without permanent wheel attachments and built in such a way that they could be stacked on top of each other.

Realizing the power (financial and otherwise) of an end-to-end business system, McLean acquired the Pan-Atlantic Steamship Company for $7 million. Pan-Atlantic was based in Alabama and had shipping and docking rights in several prime eastern port cities. Upon acquiring Pan-Atlantic he immediately started to retro-fit the ships to carry his newly designed containers.

He now had an end-to-end transportation system. He had a strong trucking company, combined with newly redesigned cargo ships, and a warehouse infrastructure to support the system and his shipper customers.

Of Malcolm McLean's "imagination/vision come to life" the *Wall Street Journal* wrote: "One of the nation's oldest and sickest industries is embarking on a quiet attempt to cure some of its own ills. The patients are the operators of coastwise and inter-coastal ships that carry dry cargoes." The *Journal* went on to say that the cure McLean was providing was really "entrepreneurial thinking," saying that business operators like McLean who were breathing new life into the shipping industry was a welcome change.

Earlier, we talked about obstacles along your navigational route and either staying the course through rough weather or making course corrections. McLean had to deal with it all. He was sued by no fewer than seven different railroads accusing him of violating the Interstate Commerce Act. The accusers said he was in violation of the section in the Act that said it "was unlawful for anyone to take control or management in a common interest of two or more carriers without getting ICC's (Interstate Commerce Commission) approval." Ultimately McLean was forced to choose between his ownership of his well-established trucking fleet or a brand new and very speculative shipping venture.

Although he was a trucker at heart, and had no real experience in the shipping industry, McLean gave up his trucking company and focused on the ship side of what was starting to be called "intermodal transportation;" a term given to the confluence of trains, trucks, and ships. He sold his 75 percent interest in McLean Trucking for $6 million in 1955 and became the owner and president of Pan-Atlantic, which he later renamed SeaLand Industries.

What Malcolm McLean imagined (i.e. thought about), and ultimately created, totally changed the maritime industry. His story is the perfect parallel to what any of us want to manifest as we go for 360° Wealth. He became aware of what he wanted, he took note of his surroundings and learned to navigate within that environment, and then he charted a course of action.

Malcolm McLean is just one example of the 360° Wealth clues and golden nuggets that can be found inside the maritime industry. This was a guy who definitely got his ship together.

My introduction to Malcolm McLean, and many others like him, all of whom left clues for me, and ultimately led to me getting The Call, started one very hot and humid day in July.

9

"We Gotta Get Out Of This Place"

"We gotta get out of this place
If it's the last thing we ever do
We gotta get out of this place
'cause (boy), there's a better life for me and you!"
(lyrics from a song written by Barry Mann / Cynthia Weil,
performed by The Animals)

The approach to the main gate is down a long, tree-lined, affluent residential street with large, sometimes ostentatious, homes on either side. Driving down this quiet lane early on a summer morning could quite easily give one the impression that what lay ahead might be pleasant, enjoyable, and perhaps even fun. In actuality, on that particular hot humid day in July, nothing was further from the truth!

As you approach the main gate and see the weathered ornate stone pillars and the wrought-iron arch emblazed with the name of the institution, one begins to realize, with some trepidation, just what one might be getting themselves into.

This particular summer morning there were six of us in the car, my parents, my three brothers, and me. And of the six of us I'm pretty sure only one of us had his butt cheeks puckering. That's because one of us wasn't going to go back home that day.

I was first introduced to Malcolm McLean and SeaLand (albeit not a personal introduction) five minutes after we parked the car and walked through the main gatehouse, known as Vickery Gate. Vickery Gate was named after Vice Admiral Howard Leroy Vickery, who was the Vice Chairman of the U.S. Maritime Commission from 1937 through 1945. Under his leadership, more than 5,500 oceangoing ships were built during World War II; a level of ship construction unmatched even to this day.

As the six of us followed the throng of other 17- and 18-year-old kids and their families, you couldn't help but notice the large house flag of SeaLand Corporation draped on the starboard (right) side of the gatehouse's interior wall. Little did I know at the time, but I was about to learn a great deal about SeaLand and come to respect and idolize Mr. McLean.

There are five Federal Academies located around the U.S. Each is a four-year college funded by the federal government and offering tuition-free education to young men and women who agree to serve their country upon graduation.

Can you name all five?

I like to ask the question because it usually stumps most people!

Three of the academies are run by the Department of Defense, one by Homeland Security, and one by the Department of Transportation. Most people can name the three largest ones, fewer can name four, and almost no one gets all five.

I'll give you a hint – Generals Ulysses S. Grant, Dwight D. Eisenhower, and George Patton all went to one of them.

Most people I quiz are able to come up with the U.S. Military Academy (aka West Point, from which the aforementioned generals graduated), the U.S. Naval Academy (aka Annapolis), and the U.S. Air Force Academy. Some are able to come up with the 4th – the U.S. Coast Guard Academy. But almost no one ever names the 5th: the U.S. Merchant Marine Academy (aka Kings Point).

As you walk though Vickery Gate you walk out of the affluent tranquil surroundings of the Village of Kings Point, a neighborhood of the rich and famous located on Long

Island, NY, and you enter the world of the United States Merchant Marine Academy, oftentimes called simply by its geographic location, "Kings Point."

And I gotta tell ya, the world inside the gate is drastically different from the one on the outside, as I was soon to find out.

As we came out on the other side of the gate we quickly caught up to a bigger mass of people, all pretty much grouped the same way. Each cluster would include a teenaged guy or girl clutching a small suitcase, usually only big enough to hold a change of clothes and some toiletries. This young (most likely scared shitless) kid would be accompanied by a parent, (or parents), some siblings (some older, but most younger), and perhaps a few other relatives like aunts, uncles, or grandparents. This day was a big day in the lives of many of these families, because just like my family, they were sending their first family member off to a federal academy.

Kings Point, like the other federal academies, was steeped in tradition, and we were about to be "indoctrinated" in the ways of "the sea," and for the next four years (if we could hack it) we were going to learn all about the heroes of our industry like Francis Gibbs, Malcolm McLean, Admiral Vickery, and a whole bunch of others.

But first the sharply uniformed student officers and just as sharply uniformed Academy staff had to get rid of all our families so that there were no witnesses to what they were about to do to us unsuspecting recent high-school graduates!

We were all herded onto a large blacktop area, that I was soon to find out was called Barney Square, named after a merchant mariner of colonial times, Commodore Joshua Barney. As we were all milling about, talking nervously about nothing, a booming voice emanated from a speaker system effectively hidden somewhere. Simultaneously, I noticed a very official looking podium, complete with the U.S. Merchant Marine Academy seal, affixed front and center, being paraded to a focal point in the square, and coming to rest at the foot of the steps of a massive building.

The booming voice says, "All Plebe Candidates form up! And would all guests please move to the outskirts of the square." At that moment what seemed like a hundred uniformed young men and women descended upon us, yelling, pointing, and gesturing us into nice neat rows and columns. There were over 450 of us assembled on Barney Square that July day and our amateurish formation covered the entire square. We were instructed (no, more like ordered) to place our bags at our feet in front of us and to remain absolutely silent as we were about to addressed by our superiors.

One at a time we were addressed by several men and women all dressed in the most pristine dress-white uniforms I had ever seen. The gold on their shoulder boards signified their respective rank, which at the time was all Greek to me. Each of their polished brass belt buckles glistened in the bright sun and was in stark contrast to the sheen of the black bills of their clean white hats. It felt like it was 100° that day, but not a single one of these perfectly attired drill instructors showed any reaction to the heat.

As we were standing erect – or at least as erect as we knew how to stand at that point – we were informed, in no uncertain terms, about a few things: (1) no fewer than 1/3 of the people assembled on Barney Square that day would not be here by the end of the first school year, (2) most likely ½ of the people around us would not be here four years from now at graduation, (3) from this day forward, and until proclaimed otherwise, we were no longer hotshot high-school graduates, but Plebe Candidates; the lowest form of being possible in the Academy system. In the days of the Holy Roman Empire a plebe was the absolute lowest-class citizen; hence the origin of the term. On this

July day we were proclaimed lower than low. We weren't even accepted as Plebes yet!

The fourth and final thing we learned was something we all knew was always inevitable, but it didn't really sink in until the Regimental Commander said it out loud – "Plebe Candidates, you're now mine!"

The voice continued: "Would all family and guests please leave the Academy grounds. It's time for us to undertake the job of turning these candidates into Plebes and accepted members of our regiment.

"Family and guests, wave goodbye to your Plebe Candidate. The next time you see him or her they will be accepted members of the Regiment of Midshipmen.

"Plebe Candidates, as your family and guests depart the Academy grounds, your eyes are to remain front, and squarely on me!"

And with those words the game was on!

For the next several weeks we Plebe Candidates were constantly reminded just how low on the totem pole we were. The Academy called this "training" Indoctrination or "Indoc" for short. A day of Indoc commenced promptly at 4:50 a.m. (0450) and lasted until well after 10 p.m. (2200). Each morning (technically the middle of the night) the

Drill Instructors, "affectionately" known as Pushers, would stampede down the linoleum hallway of our dorm (technically known as the barracks) yelling and banging on the metal transoms above our doors. They never bothered to knock or bang on the barracks doors because they were always open. The only time we were allowed to close our doors was when we were dressing.

All through Indoc we ran multiple miles, marched in formation with our M1 rifles, learned to get undressed, take a shower, and get dressed again in under five minutes, practiced basic seamanship, and learned the proper way to fold our underwear!

We marched in formation to each meal, eating with our backs perfectly straight and sitting only on the front six inches of our chairs and eating in complete silence. You could hear a fork drop during our Indoc meals; and you often did, much to regret of the Plebe who dropped it because he or she would definitely be called to task later for such an egregious mistake.

We also endured a lot of "Plebe Beats." A Plebe Beat is a Pusher's wet dream and a Plebe's nightmare. It's a non-physical, but extremely aggressive verbal assault – where the Pusher (or several Pushers) would stand inches from your face and ask all sorts of questions about the Academy and maritime history. And when you didn't have the correct answer (which was practically 100% of the time) they would hurl all sorts of insults and insinuations at you (surprisingly though, never anything about your Mama!). To compound this nightmarish effect, a Plebe Beat would always take place as we were standing, ram-rod straight, with our backs against the wall and our chins pressed firmly against our chests. This bodily position was known as a "brace" and it became a staple of our existence during Indoc.

Indoc ended the day the rest of the Regiment arrived back on campus. Up to this point it was only we Plebes (actually STILL just Plebe Candidates) and the Pushers, who were all sophomores and juniors, and the Regimental Officers, who were all seniors. Now, just like there was a special name for us "low life" freshmen (Plebe Candidates), sophomores, juniors, and seniors were called something else as well. Collectively they were all known as Upper Classmen. Individually, sophomores, juniors, and seniors were known as Third Classmen (3/C), Second Classmen (2/C), and First Classmen (1/C), respectively.

The entire look, feel, and energy of the Academy changed the day the rest of the Regiment returned. The Pushers seemed to morph back into "normal" people who were now concerned about their class schedules and extra-curricular activities. Academy life seemed to slow down a bit, become a bit more predictable, and a little less stressful. I say a little less stressful because, as Plebe Candidates, we still had no privileges and a lot of restrictions. We still had to march in formations of at least five people everywhere we went. If you were heading to class and you couldn't find a formation of other Plebes to join, or you couldn't muster up four other Plebes to create a formation, then you had to run. We also had a very heavy class load with several professors intent on making good on the Regimental Commander's Barney Square prediction about attrition come true!

One area of Academy life that loosened up a great deal was our meals in the mess hall. During Indoc we sat, literally, on the edge of our seats eating in complete silence. When the Regiment returned we were allowed to talk, and music was played during each meal.

The music that was played during meals at Kings Point was an integral part of the fabric of the Academy experience. Like much of what went on at the Academy the RBU (Radio Broadcast Unit) was run by midshipmen. In a sound-proof room high above and overlooking the entire mess hall the midshipmen who were apart of the RBU spun records (yes, vinyl records) for our mealtime enjoyment. Now granted, you were at the mercy of the particular musical taste of the person spinning the tunes, because they were in complete control, but as a Plebe, any music was better than no music, and because of our overall age group (college-aged kids) and the time period (early 80's), most of the music was rock, which was cool with me.

I'll never forget the first time I heard what was loosely referred to as "The Midshipmen's National Anthem." I had never heard the song before and after hearing the words and experiencing the effect it had on the entire regiment I garnered a whole new inner strength.

The first time I heard it was at lunch. I can't remember what was served that day but I'm sure it was something short of good. In my opinion, the mess hall only served about two decent lunches – burgers and tacos. I don't think either of those was being served that day. Anyway, the instrumental lead-in to the song starts. It starts out with a hard but very simple bass beat and then the bass is joined by a single tap on a cymbal. At this point it's obvious the song will build up to something really strong.

Within seconds after the bass begins I see the faces of the upperclassmen around me start to light up. They obviously know this song, and I can tell something fun and exciting

79

is about to start. As the lead singer begins to sing people all around me are banging their fists on the table; their grins getting wider at each new beat.

The lead singer begins with the lyrics:

"In this dirty old part of the city
Where the sun refused to shine
People tell me there ain't no use in tryin'"

I'm now starting to feel the beat and I'm definitely getting caught up in the energy of all the people around me, but I still can't put two and two together and understand why this song has the entire regiment practically jumping out of their seats.

Three more verses follow the first, and I can tell from the lyrics and energy of the fourth verse that the lead singer and the song are building toward a riveting chorus, because the fourth verse really pumps you up:

(Yeah!) He's been workin' so hard
(Yeah!) I've been workin' too, baby
(Yeah!) Every night and day
(Yeah, yeah, yeah, yeah!)

And then the entire regiment shouts the chorus at the top of their lungs, and it all comes together for me.

Chorus:

We gotta get out of this place
If it's the last thing we ever do
We gotta get out of this place
'cause girl, there's a better life for me and you!

The first time the chorus is repeated I'm still kind of in awe of the heart-pounding energy and infectious enthusiasm from the people around me, but by the time the chorus is repeated for the third time I'm right in there shouting, "We gotta get out of this place, If it's the last thing we ever do!"

Many years later I understood that this type of energy, what I'll just call for now "shared energy," is a key component of wealth. And it's a combination of components like this that make True Wealth a 360° ordeal.

The shared energy we midshipmen had when the RBU played "our anthem" was not because we all hated Kings Pont and couldn't wait to get out of there. Sure, some kids there did really hate the place, but they usually weren't around at the end for graduation. And don't get me wrong, there were days when I truly hated the place. But I got over, or through, those times pretty quickly. No, our shared energy, and the reason that song resonated so strongly with

81

us was because we knew we were all in this together. And we also knew there was a way better life after graduation because of the shit we were going through now!

From that day forward I had a new sense of purpose. I had an even more intense hunger to learn about the maritime industry; its history, its leaders, and its innovators. I don't know if I would have absorbed as much knowledge and information as I did about the true geniuses of the industry like Malcolm McLean and the creation of SeaLand had I not been swept up by the shared energy of a group of people all with a common goal.

We all knew we wanted to get out of that place. And we all knew the road (or course) to do so was through the academics and regimental system. Each of us set about charting our own course to get what we wanted – a B.S. degree, a U.S. Coast Guard merchant mariner's license, a commission in the Naval Reserve, and ultimately -- though I'm sure we didn't know it at the time – a path to 360° Wealth.

To get all that, we had to get out of that place, if it was the last thing we ever did. Because we knew, armed with our Kings Point education and all the experiences, there was such a great life waiting for us!

Let's add Charting a Course to our 360° Wealth propeller. Here's what it looks like so far

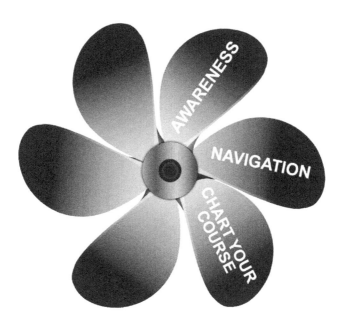

Speaking of getting out of that place, it was only about a year and a half after nervously standing on Barney Square listening to the Regimental Commander's "attrition prediction" (which unfortunately came true for many of my Barney Square shipmates), that I, too, was out of there – gone from Kings Point!

10

Your Crew

My grandfather came into the spare bedroom and woke us up around 4 a.m. Outside it was that "darkest before the dawn" type of dark. The crickets were still chirping but otherwise it was dead still everywhere outside. It was the perfect time and perfect conditions to be making our escape.

When my grandfather entered the room, Mike Booth and I were both sound asleep but still we managed to jump out of bed two seconds after my grandfather cracked the door. I think we were both super excited to be fleeing the country!

Mike and I got dressed in our crisp, recently cleaned and pressed Service Dress Blue uniforms. We made sure our brass Naval Reserve eagle pins were perfectly aligned over our breast pockets, our ties had an exact double Windsor knot, our belt buckles had no fingerprints or smudges, and our shoes still had that spit shine. Rumor had it that we might be subject to a personal appearance inspection and we didn't want anything to jeopardize our grand plan.

As we walked into the family room of my grandparents tastefully appointed, yet very comfortable, home my grandmother stepped away from the stove, sized us up, and gave us a huge reassuring smile. At least we'd passed her inspection, which I knew from past experience could be tougher than an evaluation by any so-called authority.

The smell of fresh country eggs, hickory-smoked bacon and homemade buttermilk biscuits filled the house. When I first woke up that morning I didn't think there was any way I could keep anything down, but that was before my stomach remembered what it was like to dine at 108 Elm Street in Prairie View, Texas. Mike and I hopped into dining-room chairs and devoured all that was set before us. And I guess our un-spoken rationale for inhaling second helpings was that we would need a little extra energy to get through this day. We had no idea what really lay ahead of us, but we were determined to find out.

Mike and I, and about 300 of our fellow classmates, had successfully made it through 18 months of the U.S. Merchant Marine Academy and now it was our turn to head out to sea.

Kings Point was unique among the five federal academies in a number of ways. Perhaps the biggest difference between KP and the other four was the fact that Kings Point crammed four years of a classroom college education into just three. Kings Pointers spend three years in the classroom on campus and a year at sea, sailing on real live merchant ships. Half of one's sophomore (Third Class) year and half of one's junior (Second Class) year were spent at sea.

Mike and I had "escaped" the Academy and all the classes, all-night study sessions, room inspections, crappy meals, and harassment from the Upperclassmen. The term "shit rolls downhill" was never so true as at Kings Point.

But as the dawn was nearing on this fine winter's day, all that BS seemed 1,000 miles away. And it quite literally was, because that morning we had awakened, not on Long Island in New York, but rather deep in the heart of Texas.

After breakfast we packed up our sea bags and the four of us; Mike, my two grandparents, and I, hopped in my grandfather's 1969 Chevy Malibu for the two-and-a-half-hour journey from the mega metropolis of Prairie View, Texas (population of about 30 -- haha) to the beautiful portside paradise (yes, a little sarcasm, once again) of Beaumont, Texas.

When we got to Beaumont we headed straight to the docks and found Pier 39. There before us stood one of the biggest man-made structures I had ever seen. Alongside the dock, in all her rusted glory, was the S.S. Del Rio. Her black hull was shiny in some spots but mostly dull and tired-looking all over. The Del Rio was one of Delta Steamship Lines' older ships. She was built at the end of 1960 and delivered to Delta Steamship lines in 1961. She had been operating in the South American and West African liner trade for over 20 years and was beginning to show the wear and tear.

The dock was already alive with activity, even though it was only a little after 8 a.m. when we arrived. Three shoreside cranes were hard at work lifting palates of flour and grain. The whir of the greased steel cables, coupled with the heavy buzz of multiple forklift engines, created sort of an industrial symphony. In time this would become music to my ears, but that morning it all just seemed like utter chaos.

It was aboard the S.S. Del Rio, my first real merchant ship, that I learned the valuable 360° Wealth lesson of team. You can call it "team," "tribe," "your people," it doesn't matter. The point is your True Wealth will involve other people; it absolutely has to. I'm going to keep to the maritime theme and call it your "crew."

What would your life look like, and how fun would it be, if there were no one else around? What would it be like if there were no one with which to share a sunny day on the beach, no one to beat at chess, and no one to brag to about your latest conquest? Or, no one who valued your product or service?

Fortunately for us, there are seven billion other people to share our world with. And therein lies the advantage -- and sometimes the challenge.

We all live (and work) within various crews, not in the merchant mariner work sense, but in the group sense. My definition of a crew, for the purposes of our discussion here, is simply a group of two or more people who recognize and celebrate a similarity, and/or have a common belief. Most of the time crews are formed subconsciously. Some examples of the crews you might be a part of include your family, work, school, and your neighborhood.

Being part of a crew is a natural instinct for human beings. In our early days we formed together in groups because our very survival depended on it. Today we still look to form groups, but for a totally different type of survival. Not necessarily life-and-death survival, but for social, economic, and/or spiritual survival. We seek these crews because they give us our identity and they offer comfort. Our crews get us through the tough times and give us someone to celebrate the good times with.

Why do you think Facebook has become so popular? It offers us the ability to instantly become a member of a crew.

If you think about it, you are a member of multiple crews all at once. For example, as you were growing up, you were a member of your family crew. This crew might have included your mother, your father, and your brothers and sisters. Simultaneously, you were a member of the kid crew within your family. This crew would have included you, your brothers and your sisters, and you were either a member of the male family member crew or the female family member crew.

Expanding out, your family was probably a member of the school crew, and within that crew you might have been a member of the baseball, softball, or soccer team crew.

Understanding what crews are and how they are formed is an important part of creating and living a 360° Wealth lifestyle. Crews are directly related to how you think about yourself. If you understand the power of a crew from a 360° Wealth perspective you'll begin to realize how best to use this human concept. If you can begin to think of crews as 100% inclusive and never exclusive you will be well on your way to tremendous wealth. In other words, 360° Wealth crews are never formed or joined simply to keep someone out.

This is a very important concept. Because if you recall the definition of a crew -- a group of two or more people who recognize and celebrate a similarity, and/or have a common belief -- this, by definition, means that you could be welcomed into any crew (again oftentimes this happens subconsciously) just by thinking of yourself in a certain way. Because when you think a certain way you project yourself a certain way and this is picked up by the crew.

Here's a key point – The ability to move into and out of various crews is a huge key to 360° Wealth.

Wow, let's think about this in the bigger picture…

What if you lived in a world where everyone thought about themselves in such a way that they could be invited to join any crew at any time? If that happened with multiple people on a constant and regular basis, we would have so many people who were members of so many crews simultaneously that the world would become one huge mega-crew.

At that point there would be no perceived differences between people, and when you eliminate perceived differences between people you eliminate one of the root causes of all strife and conflict.

So, can you see why understanding crews, how they work, and the way you think about yourself is so important?

True Wealth – it's a team sport. Having your support people, people who you can call on and people who have your back, is extremely important. And it's equally important to understand that you'll never be a member of every crew, but you can still have a relationship with them.

Okay, that said, let's get back to Pier 39 in Beaumont, TX.

I looked up at the giant ship before me and wondered how they ever got a thing that big to move, much less sail across the world on the seven seas. Then I realized I was going to have to haul my sea-bag up a staircase (technically called a gangway) of about 100 steps, and, because the ship was empty, it was riding high alongside the dock and the gangway was practically vertical!

Just then I noticed this monster of a guy lumbering down the gangway with a big smile on his face and pointing at me.

"Hey cadet, hold on, I'll give you a hand with dat."

He shouted up to another guy on deck, "Send dat bucket down with da crane."

The next thing I knew a huge bucket came over the side of the ship and landed right at the big guy's feet. He said to me, "Throw dat bag in dare and we'll haul it up. You da engine cadet? I'm Bennie, the Q-Med."

"Q-Med" was the way most people identified the "QMED," which stood for Qualified Member of the Engine Department.

Over the course of the next 45 days Bennie and I would become pretty close. We did a lot of work around the ship together and he taught me a lot. That early morning in January, when Bennie came topside and saw a cadet in his nicely pressed uniform with the engineer's propeller embroidered on my lapels, he knew instinctively that he wanted to help me and that we were part of the same crew.

When I first boarded that ship I was immediately identified by, and subliminally included in, several crews. Because I was an engineer I was immediately accepted as a part of the engineer's crew. I was a Kings Point cadet, so I was automatically a part of the Kings Point crew. And since cadets were considered officers, I was also accepted into the officer crew. All of this was done almost instantaneously and without any type of application, invitation, or vetting. This is what we do naturally as humans.

As it turns out, getting my stuff on board was easy compared to what lay ahead, and if it weren't for crews -- the ones I was automatically or subconsciously admitted into, and the ones I was invited to join -- I might not have survived that trip!

As soon as I got up on deck Bennie showed me to my stateroom, which was in the forward part of the ship, directly under the bridge tower, and my workspace, which was back aft in the rear of the ship. I hauled my sea-bag up to my stateroom, quickly changed out of my uniform and got into my work clothes – a simple pair of blue coveralls with the USMMA logo patch over my right breast.

From that point on I was officially a crew member of the S.S. Del Rio.

Here's another quick example to drive home this aspect and the power of understanding your crew(s).

My relationship with my younger brothers was definitely a love-hate relationship, yet we were all a part of our family's kid crew, and we were all a part of the brother crew. I'm sure I had a very natural, stereotypical relationship that big brothers have with little brothers. Because I was the oldest of four boys, I would beat them up all the time, just because they were my little brothers and they were annoying. But there were certain times that I protected them, too.

The house we grew up in Washington DC., like a lot of houses there, had four stories. We had a kitchen, living room, dining room, etc., on one floor, bedrooms on another floor, and then we had a basement and an attic. I used to play a game with my brothers and some other neighborhood kids called Four-Floor Football. One end zone was in the basement and the other in the attic. The object of the game was to get to your end zone, with the football, without getting tackled, pummelled or beat up. As far as games made up by young boys, our game was probably pretty normal, except for our own unique twist. We used my youngest brother Phill as the football.

Now even though I'd beat my brothers mercilessly I'd never let any harm come to them from anyone else. Sometimes that was a pretty tall order. My brother Brian in particular got pretty used to his big brother sticking up for him. So comfortable, in fact, that he'd go to parties and act tough knowing that I had his back. Well, on a couple of occasions he got himself into some trouble before I had even arrived at the party. I remember a couple of times arriving at a party and finding Brian cornered somewhere with four of five guys my age ready to kick his ass for some reason, probably very well deserved, but I couldn't let that happen. No one was going to mess with my little brothers – except me!

Think about the teams, tribes, or crews that you are a part of, and think about the crews that you could or should be a part of. Remember our Ship's Wheel illustrating the six areas that support our propulsion toward 360° Wealth? Well this is one key example of the Relationship spoke.

Our 360° Wealth propeller continues to take shape; let's add another blade!

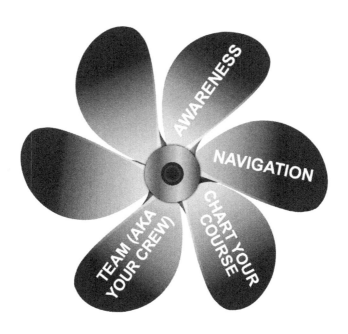

11

Getting Your Sea Legs

The second largest body of water in the world is the Atlantic Ocean. Here's some fun stats: the Atlantic Ocean covers a total area of about 41,100,000 square miles, that's about 30% of our entire planet, and about one fifth of all the water in our world.

It also separates the "Old World" from the "New World" -- the world Columbus left in 1492, and the world he wanted to get to.

In many ways, the "Old World" for those seeking wealth is like trying to live your life without a chart. Or, even more problematic, trying to live our lives in a world we think is flat, because we can't see or believe that the world is actually round.

What we need is "New World" thinking, which requires belief and faith in what you can't always readily see, and it requires getting your "sea legs." And the Atlantic is the perfect place to do it, or so I thought ....

After Mike and I had gotten our gear aboard and found our stateroom, we stripped off our Service Dress Blues, and jumped into our "boiler suits" (our work overalls). For the next 60 days our Dress Blues wouldn't see the light of day! From that day forward we were real merchant mariners and our new uniform would be jeans, teeshirts, khakis, and overalls. Properly dressed and no longer looking like airline pilots, we headed to our respective departments. Mike headed forward toward the bow of the ship and reported to the First Mate and I headed aft (the rear of the ship) to find the engine room and the Chief Engineer.

We set sail that evening and our first "romantic" port of call was to be Houston; a grand total of about 100 nautical miles and a short overnight trip cruising at about 10 knots. But hey, I was finally aboard ship and actively embarking on my new career. I was beyond excited, but also scared to death!

After spending a year and half at the Academy on the campus on Long Island, New York, going to class from sun up to sundown five days a week, and studying hard at night and on the weekends, I was excited to finally be at sea. Even if at this point I hadn't even made it out of the state of Texas.

But at the same time, I was sacred shitless of getting seasick!

Now tell me if you can relate to this ....

How many times in your life, have you been off-the-charts excited about what you're doing, and at the same time scared shitless about "what you're doing?"

Well good, because if you didn't have those diametrically opposing thoughts and feelings going on I'd say either, one, you weren't human, or two, and more likely, you weren't doing something that really excited you.

This duality of being totally excited and totally scared is totally natural. So how do we handle it? What did I do in this case?

Well, went ahead and get seasick, of course!

I had made it to Houston unscathed. After having our first meal under way, a nice steak dinner with mashed potatoes and mixed vegetables with apple pie ala mode for dessert, Mike and I chatted for a while in our stateroom before nodding off to sleep.

Life aboard a U.S. cargo ship is not such a bad gig, especially if you're an officer. And as cadets at the U.S. Merchant Marine Academy we were considered officers. As such, we ate in the officer's mess along with the Captain, Chief Engineer, Chief Mate, and all the other Mates and Assistant Engineers. On most merchant ships, especially U.S. flag merchant ships, food is considered part of your pay, and the food aboard most merchant ships is very good; you can order anything you want and eat as much as you want. Every meal was served to us by a white-gloved Steward and prepared by an entire staff in the galley (the ship's kitchen).

Normally every officer (and we cadets) aboard a merchant ship has his or her own stateroom, but on the Del Rio they were using each cadet's stateroom for storage. The Del Rio hadn't carried cadets in a while and the crew had gotten used to having the cadet rooms as extra space. So, poor us, we were told we'd have to share a room and we'd be berthing in the Owner's Stateroom.

Most dry-cargo ships built in the '40s, '50s and '60s were designed to carry a very small number of passengers. The Del Rio had capacity for 12 passengers. The steamship companies did this to generate extra revenue as they were hopping from port to port on their liner runs. As you can imagine, the passengers who booked trips on these types of cargo ships were a unique breed, but they absolutely loved the adventure. Typically, they were retired couples who had a lot of money, time on their hands, and wanted to see "how the other side lived." Because these voyages were typically 45 to 60 days long, and not cheap, they went to the industrial ports, not the glamor spots that the full-on passenger liners and cruise ships were calling on.

The Del Rio had 6 passenger staterooms, one of which was considered the Owner's Stateroom. The term is kind of a misnomer because Delta was a publicly traded company with lots of owners. Of course there was the CEO of the company, but he rarely, if ever, travelled overnight on any of the ships in the fleet. But regardless, the room was the biggest and best of the bunch and Mike and I were stoked to be there. At least until it became my sanctuary from Hell.

After loading the last of our foreign-bound cargo in Houston we were ready to set sail for our first overseas port. We were headed to Brazil.

Now I don't imagine many of you have sailed into or out of the Port of Houston. I mean, why would you? It's not exactly a cruise tourist's hot spot! But it is the third largest port in the U.S. and a major hub for cargo both domestic and foreign.

One of the unique things about sailing in and out of Houston is travelling the Houston Ship Channel; fifty miles of inland waterway that connects the various docks, terminals, and berths in Houston with the Gulf of Mexico.

Under normal circumstances, sailing the Houston Ship Channel is like riding in a Cadillac, sitting on a bed of feathers, cruising down a freshly paved, totally flat highway, while getting a back rub from a masseuse. In other words, it ain't rough at all. So naturally, that's when and where I got seasick!

I was so scared of getting seasick, and so intent on NOT getting seasick, that I literally talked myself into getting seasick! We had made it through the Houston Ship Channel and were now in the relatively calm waters of the Gulf of Mexico, but I was already starting to feel queasy. And by the time we hit the open waters of the Atlantic Ocean I was full-on seasick.

C.E. ("Al") Allen was the First Assistant Engineer aboard the Del Rio. This was one old crusty bastard if there ever was one. And if he's still alive (which I gotta doubt) he'd smile with pride at that description.

The First Assistant Engineer, usually just called The First aboard ship, is the second most senior person in the engine department; just under the Chief Engineer. The Chief is ultimately responsible for anything and everything in the engine room, but The First really runs the show.

Al was a hellava guy. He had graduated from the U.S. Merchant Marine Academy (my school) in 1944, and he had been at sea pretty much ever since. He stood about 5'9" and couldn't have weighed more than 150 pounds, but he still had a belly that lopped over his belt. He had a full head of white hair and a white beard just like St. Nick. A Marlboro cigarette was constantly protruding from his mouth. I think he smoked close to three packs a day! He only drank in port, seemed to eat only every now and then, and every other word out of his mouth was an F-bomb! A real merchant mariner if there ever was one.

And he saved my life!

Well it least it felt that way at the time.

This crusty old sailor saw an 18-year-old kid who was having a hard time getting his sea legs. After he stopped laughing at how pathetic I looked day in and day out as we crossed the Atlantic toward Brazil, he made sure I survived.

Every morning, as I'd gingerly wobble my way back aft from my Owner's Stateroom to the engineering quarters, he'd allow me to recline in his office and sip on a Coke – about the only thing that actually agreed with my stomach those first few days. Then he'd assign me the easiest task available that day, and he'd always partner me with the best unlicensed guy who would really do all the work. He hid me from The Chief, a good old boy from New Orleans who didn't go to an Academy but rather worked his way up the ranks and didn't have much use for us Academy cadets. He thought we all had it too easy.

But Al knew his way around a ship. And he knew how to deal with all the politics, and all the other bullshit. And he taught me a lot about business and life in general. In so many ways, he had his sea legs.

The first thing I realized as we got under way and were making way was that there is a hellava lot that goes on aboard a ship and the engineers never get a break. The Chief Mate, other Mates, and the rest of the deck department are busy in port loading and unloading cargo but for the engineers there's always something going on. And Al had it all under control. It didn't matter if the ship was pitching and yawing in 20-foot swells, as it was on our way to Brazil, or if all hell was breaking loose because a main boiler unexpectedly shut down; Al took it all in stride. He'd just light up another Marlboro, let out a stream of profanity that could make milk curdle, and then get on about his business. A very valuable skill for an entrepreneur, as I would note later in my business life.

Each day as we got closer and closer to our first foreign port, the little port town of Maceió, Brazil, I started to feel less seasick and more like myself again. Probably if for no other reason than I knew the damn ship would have to stop and I could plant my feet once again on terra firma!

The morning we were scheduled to arrive I woke at 5:30 a.m. (0530) and slipped out of our stateroom without waking Mike. He, by the way, had made it all the way across without so much as a bout of indigestion and was sound asleep, having just worked the 12-4 watch (midnight to 4 a.m.). I was heading aft to the engine room to help The First maneuver the ship into the dock.

If you're a maritime novice, you might be wondering, what do the engineers have to do with maneuvring a ship into dock? You're probably thinking doesn't the captain and the guys on the bridge dock the ship? Well they do, AND, for a ship as old as the Del Rio, maneuvring is a multi-department operation.

Older ships, ships built before the mid 1970's, and in particular steamships, maneuvered in a tag team between the navigation bridge and the engine control platform. The bridge did most of the navigation work of maneuvring, and steered the ship alongside the dock, but it was the engine room that provided the desired speed and ship direction, either forward (moving ahead) or astern (moving backward). The bridge relayed the desired speed and desired direction to the engine room over the Engine Order Telegraph, then it was up to the engine room to give them what they wanted.

As primitive as it might sound, all we did on the engine-control platform was open valves to let steam into the turbines. We'd open the "Ahead" valve and let steam flow one way to move the ship forward, then we'd close that valve, and open the "Astern" valve and let steam flow in the opposite direction to move the ship backward. It might sound simple, but proper speed, and proper direction were so critical to safe vessel maneuvering that this was a responsibility given specifically to The First.

As we approached Maceió early that morning, I was down below with Al to observe maneuvring from the engineer's perspective. About half-way into the process Al told me to take over and bring her in! Nervous as hell, I put my sweaty palms on the valve wheels. The next engine order came down from the bridge and I rapidly closed the Ahead valve and lunged toward the Astern valve to slow the ship down. So far so good.

We continued to maneuver for the next half hour or so and bumped the dock around 0800. The last line was secured at 0836 and the Finished With Engines (FYE) bell was send down to us. We marked the time in our engine log book, signed it and headed topside for breakfast.

That morning when I came topside and walked forward toward the officer's mess for breakfast it felt like a new day. The sun was already high and bright in the sky, the air smelled crisp and clean, and most importantly the ship wasn't moving under my feet! We were tied up, stationary, a gangway away from dry land. Life was good!

And I was starving! My diet coming across had been a whole lot of bland foods like rice, bread, toast, oatmeal, and meat with no kind of sauce; oh, and a lot of Al's Coke! That morning I think I ordered one of everything on the menu. And man, did it taste good!

We spent about five days in Maceió. The Mates were super busy supervising the unloading of pallets with bags of grain and loading pallets with Brazilian coffee. Mike and I got ashore a few times and had a great time exploring the local culture (mostly the bars)!

We set sail again on the evening of that fifth day, heading to the west coast of Africa. What lay ahead was about 10 days of full steaming in the wide open, and often rough Atlantic Ocean. But now I had my sea legs!

Amazingly, for the rest of that voyage, some 50 days, I never once got seasick; and we hit some pretty rough waters. To this day, whenever I set out on any type of vessel (big or small) I get a rumbling in the pit of my stomach for about 30 seconds, then nothing at all as my sea legs kick back in.

Getting seasick in the Houston Ship Channel, while embarrassing to admit to my mariner brothers and sisters, was probably the greatest gift as it relates to me becoming 360° Wealthy. Not only did I learn that no situation is permanent, I learned how to deal with and survive stress and discomfort. I also learned a great deal about partnership, mentorship, and basic caring for your fellow man. My crew had my back.

There was one other key ingredient that helped me survive those seasick days and it's an ingredient that's like the glue that holds all your wealth aspirations together and moving forward. I also, NEVER would have gotten The Call without it.

Wanna know what that is?

Sure you do!

Here's a quick story ....

12

Don't Know, Don't Care!

The second quarter of my freshmen year at Gonzaga College High School, a school that one day I hoped would be my alma mater, was a pivotal point in my understanding of how True Wealth is created, and I didn't even know it. At the time I was way too scared!

Right in the heart of Washington, DC, the school had been a bastion of all-male Catholic higher education since first established in 1821, run by Jesuit priests with iron fists and compassionate hearts.

This day my class was in Kohlmann Hall. It was going to take a little longer to get there, because I first had to figure out where the hell it was.

You might expect I would know my way around the school's numerous buildings. But no, it seemed like every other day I learned about a new hidden passageway, staircase, route, or classroom. This was one of those days.

As a freshman, I had quickly learned the most effective way not to show my ignorance was to find another freshman who was in the same class and follow him, hoping he knew the way to the new classroom. Asking an upperclassman how to get there was out of the question as that would open me up to ridicule for weeks to come.

So that morning, I followed this skinny, geeky kid who I thought (no, I hoped and prayed) was in my class. It was a calculated gamble, but one I had to take because I didn't have any other options at the time.

As I followed him "blindly" up and down short flights of stairs, through narrow corridors, and past other classrooms already filling up for the next period, I contemplated my fate should I arrive at the wrong classroom.

Should this, I'm sure very nice, but also very geeky, kid lead me to the wrong place, I'd of course have no one but myself to blame. But my real concern was having to re-start my classroom search, eventually arrive late, be snickered at by my fellow freshmen classmates who had somehow miraculously found the right room, and worse yet, get detention!

Detentions, also known as "jug" at Gonzaga, were an hour of "silenced group solitary confinement" (an oxymoron if ever there was one). You were placed in a room with fellow students -- freshmen, sophomores, juniors, and seniors, and forced to sit in absolute silence, while being watched over by the Dean of Discipline.

The Jesuits, in their infinite wisdom, realized that having a young man sit in total silence, basking in his own self-humiliation, while being stared at and telepathically humiliated by his fellow students, was way more effective than any other form of punishment, including, I think, physical torture. At least that's the way I felt at the ripe old age of 14!

On this particular day, to add potential insult to potential injury, the class I was praying to get to on time, to avoid ridicule, embarrassment and detention, was being taught by none other than the school's Dean of Discipline, the Right Reverend Father H. Cornell Bradley!

Father Bradley was one tough SOB! (Forgive me Lord for using the term SOB, but I think even you would agree that in Fr. Bradley's case the term is spot on!) Rumour was that he was a former Alabama State Trooper turned priest. How and why that transformation ever took place, I'm sure only The Almighty knows!

This particular class was my second Theology class of the year. Over the course of my education at Gonzaga I would take a total of 16 Theology classes, one every quarter for four years. It was a Catholic school after all, I guess it was the least they could do!

Through what seemed like divine intervention, I made it to Fr. Bradley's class on time. Though through no help, by the way, from the nerdy, geeky, kid I was following. It turned out he was headed for a different class, but fortunately my Kohlmann Hall class was right next door.

I flew in the door five seconds in front of Fr. Bradley. This gave me just enough time to drop my books on an unoccupied desk and plop down in my seat before Fr. Bradley arrived. He entered the room, stood perfectly erect, placed his hands on his hips, scanned the room with those penetrating eyes of his, and motioned for us to stand for the class' opening prayer.

I would guess that 95% of all my classes at Gonzaga stared with a prayer -- usually the Our Father or a Hail Mary, at the end of which the teacher would say "Saint Aloysius Gonzaga…" and we students would say in unison, "Pray for us."

The opening prayer complete, Fr. Bradley motioned for us to take our seats. Then he just stood there and stared at us for what seemed like an eternity. It was probably only about five seconds, but Fr. Bradley had that effect on young men! I'll never forget what he said next.

In his deep, baritone voice, Fr Bradley said, "That day, on the banks of the River Jordan, did Jesus really feed 5,000 people with just two fish and five loaves of bread?"

I remember stealing a quick glance around the room and thinking to myself what I imagined every other boy was thinking at that very moment -- was this some kind of trick question? Of course he did! He was Jesus, wasn't he?

No one raised their hand to answer, because no one wanted to incur the wrath of Fr. Bradley by supplying a wrong answer to such a simple question. Instead, like sheep about to be slaughtered, we all waited for Fr. Bradley to call on one unlucky soul.

But he didn't call on any of us! He paused briefly, then I saw the slightest smile crack on his hardened face.

He repeated the question.

"That day, on the banks of the River Jordan, did Jesus really feed 5,000 people with just two fish and five loaves of bread?"

This time, he immediately followed his question by saying, in an ever louder and booming voice:

"DON'T KNOW, DON'T CARE!"

Then just as quickly, he added, "At a wedding in Cana, did Jesus turn water into wine?"

"DON'T KNOW, DON'T CARE!"

Finally, he shouted, "Did Jesus ever actually walk on water?"

"DON'T KNOW, DON'T CARE!"

We all just sat there, staring at this former southern state trooper turned ordained priest, dressed in his midnight-black trousers and shirt, with the two-inch width of his white clerical collar the only color contrast of his priestly uniform. What did I think?

Is this guy going to Hell? And more importantly is he going to take all of us with him!

I know it sounds dramatic, but what transpired that day in a high school classroom in downtown Washington, DC had a profound impact on my life. That experience, in fact the context of that entire religion class that quarter, left me with some great clues.

Thank God (pun intended), Fr. Bradley didn't leave us hanging with his apparent blasphemy that day. He went on to say that the particulars and exact details of Jesus' miracles were not what was important.

What was important was that in all of Jesus' miracles he was showing us that he was "the son of God," and even more importantly, that it was our faith, our belief in the idea that Jesus was the son of God and a part of the Holy Trinity, that made us unique.

Fr. Bradley went on to tell us young, impressionable, 14-year-old high-school freshmen, that we Catholics had a certain belief, and we had faith that this belief was true. In fact, he said, this was the very definition of "faith," a deep-seated belief that something is true, and not requiring additional proof beyond any doubt of how or why it is.

Fr. Bradley also told us not everyone in the world had our faith, or believed that Jesus was the son of God, or believed in the Holy Trinity. He said that was okay with him and it should be okay with us.

He said that just because we Catholics had a certain faith, that didn't make others wrong, or us better than anyone else.

Although I didn't realize it at that moment, hearing this was a major clue for me! I had just been exposed to a new and improved way to think and I had been given another piece to my puzzle.

In order to build your best ship and set sail on your wealth voyage to your New World (i.e. a life that totally lights you up), I believe it's critical to have some faith.

There are concepts, ideas, and other's beliefs that I'm sure you've been exposed to. Find the clues for you. I guarantee they are there.

The fact that you have been exposed to, heard about, and perhaps even seen other points of view does not make them right and you wrong, or vice versa. Find what resonates with you and incorporate that into your beliefs, if they support you. Then have faith that you're on the right track.

When you get your ship together and start to use the blades in our Wealth propeller, opportunities and navigational courses will open up for you.

To create wealth in a 360° way you need to have faith in your actions and in eventually getting to your destination.

Remember, faith is a deep-seated belief that something is true, and it doesn't require additional proof beyond any doubt of how or why it is.

Said a slightly different way, having faith in something means that you simply accept it for what it is, and you don't need to know why it is in order to believe in it and use it.

Even if you don't consider yourself a religious or spiritual person, you have deep-seated beliefs and faith in lots of things. You have a belief and faith in gravity. This is why you don't walk off tall buildings!

Most of us don't really know how or why gravity works, but we all believe in it and accept it on faith.

Our current banking system is something else we have a belief in and faith around. Most of us don't really understand how money is electronically debited from our bank account, or how our pay check gets direct deposited, but we believe those transfers happen, and we spend money as if they "truly" did happen.

Are you ready to move further down the road to creating the world the way you desire it to look? Together, we can go step-by-step. What is being revealed to you is a system and method that works brilliantly.

Will my system be the exact, perfect, "no stone left unturned," "no need to alter" system for you? Will it "metaphorically" allow you to walk on water?

"DON'T KNOW, DON'T CARE!"

Just dive in, take what works for you and discard the rest. So, turn the page and let's look at a few more puzzle pieces.

Be on the lookout for the clues!

Allow yourself to find them, and you will.

13

Underway and Making Way

A ship's voyage officially begins the moment the last line is cast off from the dock. At that point the ship is said to be "under way." A ship is under way as long as it's not at anchor, tied up, or tethered in any way. But for a ship to be "making way" it needs to be in motion by its own power – whatever that power might be – engines, oars, sails, or the like.

The same is true for you as you enter the realm of the 360° Wealthy. The minute you climb your proverbial gangway, and board your ship, by deciding what it is you want out of life you are officially "under way" and your voyage can start. But at that point you are only "under way" and not necessarily "making way." Ideally you want to be constantly making way to arrive at your various ports of call. Ports of call are my metaphor for "Outcomes."

Simply put, Outcomes are the end-game. Outcomes are where, who, or what you ultimately want to be. And ports are the perfect metaphor for us because ports, like outcomes, are destinations. Getting under way is super important, but, if you're not also making way, you'll never get to your desired outcome.

I gotta tell ya, there's nothing more eerie than a ship in the middle of the ocean at night that has lost power i.e., it is under way but not making way! When it first happens, everything goes black. Then with any luck, the emergency generators kick in and you have sparse light throughout the ship. The biggest problem still remains though; your ship is dead in the water and you're in the middle of nowhere helplessly facing whatever the power of the ocean decides to throw your way. The real bitch of the situation is that you never seem to lose power in calm seas. The shit always seems to hit the fan in rough weather! When that happens, you're still under way, but you're definitely not making way. For any sailor it's one of their worst nightmares and for the engineers aboard the ship it's a frantic scurry and massive action to get the plant back up and running.

Suffice it to say, as a sailor with the destination of 360° Wealth you pretty much want to get under way as soon as possible and you want to be making way until you get to your destination.

It's all about the desired outcomes you set for yourself, having faith that those outcomes, or something even better, will show up on the horizon, assembling your crew, and navigating toward them.

There once was a man who had a direct impact on my life and was a big reason why I decided what I wanted was to own and operate ships. Although he and I never met, his ability to constantly, consistently, and creatively make way left me with many clues and offered me many opportunities. I might even argue that had our life paths not crossed I would not have had the skills and experiences that led me to answer The Call.

In the month of May, almost 100 years ago (my, how time flies), a very elderly and semi-retired Vladimir Lenin, the ailing leader of the Communist Russian Revolution, sent a letter to Joseph Stalin, the newly appointed General Secretary of the Communist Party, instructing him and the Politburo to strike a business deal with a certain young American; thus the last line was cast off the dock, and a very unique and profitable voyage had begun. With that letter a simple "country doctor" was under way!

His final destination was reached almost 60 years later in 1981 when his company, Occidental Petroleum (aka Oxy), launched a ship called the Oxy Producer, and a crew of 17 merchant seamen and two young Merchant Marine Academy cadets (one of whom you might become very familiar with by the time you finish reading this book) set sail from Jacksonville, Florida to the Evil Empire (aka the Soviet Union), hauling the first of what would be a series of cargos the good doctor would deliver over next 20 years, conservatively generating his company more than $20 billion in revenue.

The entrepreneur behind this profitable maritime business was a short, balding man, who wore prescription glasses with lenses as thick as Coke bottles and travelled the world in his customized private Boeing 727 jet. He collected art, bred horses, drilled for oil, and built some unique ships.

He was of Jewish descent, yet was very friendly with, and did business with, the United Arab Emirates (UAE) and Muammar Gaddafi and Libya. He was a master of deals done in equal regularity in the proverbial "dark, smoke-filled rooms" of shady business establishments, as well as the Presidential suites of hotels all around the world. Surrounded by high-priced lawyers and Swiss bankers he consummated one deal after another. One was a Persian Gulf oil deal struck with an Emirate Sheik, where this entrepreneur is reported to have personally delivered $1,671,000 in a suitcase to a hotel room in the heart of London's financial district, and then sweetened the deal by depositing another $200,000 in a Swiss bank on the Sheik's behalf.

So, who is this man of international mystery, and what clues does he offer us in true 360° Wealth form? Well he's none other than Armand Hammer. A master at making way!

His father, Julius Hammer, was one of the founders of the American Communist Labor Party. Julius is rumored to have named his son "Armand" Hammer as an homage to the hammer and sickle symbols of the Soviet flag. Somewhat ironically, Armand Hammer went on to become a multimillionaire capitalist, thanks in large part to the deals he struck with the Soviet Union and other "questionable" regimes.

The adage of "it's not what you know but who you know" couldn't be more appropriate when talking about Mr. Hammer. This is a major clue to navigating the 360° Wealth waters. At the end of the day, all success involves people in some form or fashion. Today, I so often see people looking to hide behind the internet, never venturing out to make human connections. Ultimately deals are done person-to-person, and all success, including great wealth, is created one relationship at a time. You'd be surprised at how much money can be generated from just one win/win contact.

This is how Armand Hammer "set sail" and "made way" to corporate billions. And you can too, if you make use of this navigational clue. Armand Hammer maintained cordial relations with Soviet leaders for more than half a century, bringing Russia and its satellite countries all sorts of goods and services and making lots of money.

And here's another great clue – figure out how to do business with the Russians! No, just kidding. The clue I want to point out is this: never get too ideologically stuck or committed, and always keep your eye on your prize, aka your outcome. If you constantly keep in mind what you really want you will often find that the course you originally set, or the course you think you should take, is not always the best way to get there.

Hell, Armand Hammer was a card-carrying Democrat but he supported Tricky Dick (that's President Richard Nixon for those of you too young to have known him). Why? Because Hammer knew that Nixon and the Republicans were pro foreign trade. Don't over commit to a particular course of travel. Always keep your eye toward your destination and be ready and willing to course-correct.

Lenin might have gotten Hammer under way, but it was up to Hammer to make way; and the same is true for you.

When Armand Hammer took over Occidental Petroleum in the 1960's, the company had just three employees and was worth only $34,000. At that time he was nearly 60 years old and he had no experience in the oil business. Less than 10 years later, Hammer had built Occidental into a multi-national corporation worth billions. With sales of over $12 billion, the corporation ranked in the Fortune 500 as the 20th largest industrial company in the United States. It's not always what you know, but who you know!

Armand Hammer knew that one key to making way, and therefore a lot of money, was to control his costs. And it should be no different for you! Now I'm not talking about saving every penny you make, or never spending any money. No, I'm talking about living your life, and creating a wealthy 360° lifestyle much the same way Armand Hammer created and built his business empire. And never forget, 360° Wealth is never just about the money!

What did Armand Hammer do to propel his wealth? He built ships that looked and performed like other (similar) ships, but he built his ships to operate at a fraction of the cost!

Those of us who actually sailed on his "unique" ships used to say they were designed by accountants and lawyers, not naval architects.

Just so you better understand what we're talking about here, it takes a lot of ship to transport over 45,000 tons of liquid fertilizer 5,600 miles from Jacksonville, Florida to

Odessa, in the Ukraine. These ships were almost 700 feet long, almost 100 feet wide, and about 5 stories tall. They were built under the rules, regulations, and guidelines of the United States and the U.S. Coast Guard. Normally, the rules and regs would require a crew of 35-40 people to operate the ship. But because the Oxy Producer and her sister ships, the Oxy Trader, and the Oxy Grower, were designed by "accountants and lawyers" Armand Hammer was able to reduce his crew size to just 17!

Even a third-grader can do this math. If you cut your crew count in half, what do you think you do to your overall costs? You got it; Mr. Hammer figured out a way to get his cargo half way across the world at a fraction of the normal cost. Now that's what I call making way!

Now before you run out and exclaim to your business partner, employees, spouse, or significant other that your future wealth and ultimate success is imminent because all you need to do is cut your expenses in half, remember all actions have consequences. And all course corrections will lead you somewhere different. And your new course may not be any better than the old course. And, of course, 360° Wealth is about more than just money. Let's get back to the Oxy ships.

While the brilliant Mr. Hammer was flying around on his 727, striking lucrative deals with Communists and brutal dictators, those of us onboard his first (uniquely designed) chemical tanker, the Oxy Producer, were trying to tie up all the last-minute details of taking delivery of a brand-new ship from the shipyard.

Once all the "i's" were dotted and the "t's" crossed and all the shipyard workers had walked down the gangway to the dock for the last time, our fun truly began. Do you sense a note of sarcasm here?

The Oxy Producer's maiden voyage was a true bitch! First of all, when you try to run a ship of this size and complexity with a crew of just 19 people, top to bottom, you're gonna have some challenges! Now when I say 19 seamen, top to bottom, I mean in total, all accounted for, the whole nine yards, Everyone, from the Captain on down to the guy who swept the deck! Hell, there were only six people in the entire engine department, and two of us were just kids with a grand total of eight months of sailing time between us! My sailing partner AJ and I were the reason the crew total "ballooned" from 17 to 19. Normally the engine department on an Oxy ship is only four officers. Having two additional bodies was like manna from heaven for the Chief.

The Chief Engineer decided to split us up into 2 groups of three and we stood what are called 6 and 6 watches. This meant that three of us stood watch in the engine room for 6 hours, then we had 6 hours off (while the other group stood watch), then we were back on watch for another 6 hours – "rinse and repeat."

Now, lest this sound easy, or at the very least do-able, think about trying to live your life six hours at a time. Work for 6 hours, take 6 hours off, then jump back on your business for 6 hours, and so on and so forth all day, every day. I'd bet you'd be a basket case after two days! Try doing it every day for over TWO WEEKS! And remember, when you knocked off your shift you still had to wind down, get something to eat, hop in the shower, and then get to bed. By the time you did all that you had (maybe) 4 ½ hours to sleep. Oh, and by the way, we weren't just sitting behind a desk "shooting the shit" for 6 hours while on watch. We were flying all over the engine room answering equipment alarms and troubleshooting the machinery. You know how new restaurants have "soft openings" so they can work out the bugs? Well, taking delivery of a brand new ship from the shipyard is a lot like opening a new restaurant, and her maiden voyage is like a "soft opening" except when you're under way it's the real deal, you're in the middle of the ocean, shit's flying all over the place and you can't go crying to your momma – cause she ain't there!

Oh, and I almost forgot what made it even more fun for the six of us ....

Because this ship was dreamed up by accountants and lawyers, it was designed with the specifications of a tugboat, not a real ship. This is why the U.S. Coast Guard let us sail with a crew of just 17 (plus 2 cadets). And, these "brilliant" accountants and lawyers figured out that in order to make everything "work" they should design the thing to have two separate engine rooms, each independent of the other. Each engine room was three stories of machinery space located below the main deck engine control room. So, it wasn't uncommon, during our maiden "soft opening" voyage, to be all the way down on the lowest (port side) engine room deck working on a problem, when an alarm would go off on a piece of machinery located on the lowest (starboard side) engine room deck! So you'd have to haul your dog-tired butt up three flights of stairs, run across the engine control room, and descend down a different three flights of stairs to see what the trouble was. After three of these days I was beginning to re-think my choice of careers! All thanks to an elderly country doctor and some serious creativity when it comes to "making way"!

So what clues did I glean ...?

First of all, never let your creativity be stymied. Just because something has never been done before is no reason why you can't or shouldn't do it. The most important thing to "get" as you get your ship together and become wealthy in a 360° sort of way, is to know where you want to go. If you know your destination, and then let your creativity flow, then you can figure out a way to get there. All you gotta do is start – get under way, then keep moving toward your desired port – i.e., keep making way!

Once under way, just keep going from port to port, outcome to outcome!

After I decided I wanted to own and operate ships, and that desire passed the "urgent want litmus test" because it totally lit me up, I slowly began to "make way", and each step I took brought me closer and closer to The Call.

And the first port on this particular 360° Wealth voyage – my first most desired outcome – was to find John Morris!

So I grabbed hold of my ship's wheel and set sail for my desired port of call. After all, I figured it was about time!

Ahoy mate-ies, we've uncovered the buried treasure of the fifth propeller blade – Outcomes!

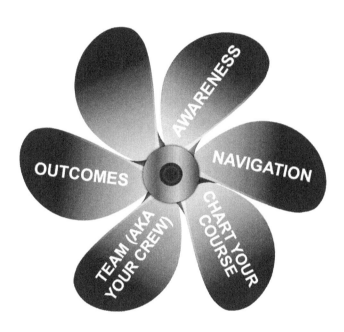

14

Everything In Time

So I'm on a quest to find this guy, John Morris, and at this point I'm not even sure if he's a real guy. His character is kind of a mystery man to me at this point. But I know I gotta find him because I'm sure he's the key to my most desired outcome – to own and operate ships.

Remember the ship's wheel...

The pursuit of my ship-owning outcome, and in fact any 360° Wealth endeavour, is all about your mastery of time and your thoughts. Let's dive a little deeper into both of these. First time ....

My seasick days forever behind me, and the S.S. Del Rio and its crew a fond memory, I found myself on the S.S. Ruth Lykes, calling on ports in the Mediterranean Sea.

We had been at sea for nearly seven days, slow steaming from Algeria to Alexandria, Egypt and Port Said. The Chief Mate estimated we would spend about three days in port, based on the cargo we had to unload and the dock crane capacity of the port.

Port Said is an Egyptian city at the northern end of the Suez Canal, on the Mediterranean Sea. Built in 1859 to house men working on the Suez Canal, it has been a major trading port for centuries, and is a hub of international commerce. We were delivering grain to be distributed throughout northern Africa on behalf of the U.S. Agency For International Development (USAID).

It was a rather gloomy day as we made our approach to the port area. I sprinted up the three decks from the engine room to the main deck to get a glimpse of the port and city as we arrived. There were cargo ships everywhere! The port was bustling with activity already, at 8:00 in the morning.

As we made our gradual approach to the Outer Anchorage, I could see the skyline of the city of Alexandria and the iconic Islamic-style Suez Canal Authority Building, with its green domes set on the coastline.

I had a lot of eager anticipation arriving at this port, because I had never been to Egypt and I was excited to see what were considered one of the Seven Wonders of the World, the pyramids at Giza. I had been on pins and needles since I joined the ship in New Orleans and found out that Alexandria would be a port of call. The pyramids were truly an engineering feat. Built around 2500 BC, the largest of the three pyramids at Giza was comprised of more than two million blocks of limestone, granite, hardened mud, each weighing over two and a half tons! Archaeologists estimate it took over 20,000 people and more than 20 years to build one pyramid. I couldn't wait to see them in person!

Normally during a port arrival I'd be in the bowels of the ship, in the engine control room, standing an arrival watch and working with the other engineering officers to maneuver the ship to the dock. However, today the First Assistant Engineer said I could go topside to see the sights of port and city as we arrived.

I could only imagine how my fellow officers on the bridge felt as we maneuvered in, because as I said, there were literally ships everywhere and there seemed to be no rhyme or reason as to why so many were anchored or why they were scattered about so.

As I stood at the ship's rail, gazing at the hustle and bustle of the port and the city behind it, I felt the gentle rumbling of the ship below my feet. We were slowing down. Worse, I could tell by the vibration of the deck that we were going in reverse, aka "astern," or "backing down" in sailor-speak. Before I could figure out why we were stopping and no longer approaching the port, I heard the unmistakable explosion of metal on metal as the ship's anchor was released from the hawse pipe. The ship shook violently as each 300-pound link of chain toppled in to the water.

It only takes about three minutes to drop anchor on a typical cargo ship, but dropping anchor that day seemed like an eternity because with each shot of chain that went into the water I knew the pyramids were getting farther and farther away from me.

My worst fears were confirmed when I went into the Officer's Mess for breakfast and overheard the Captain talking to the Chief Mate about how long we would probably be anchored. Turns out it's fairly common at Port Said to anchor and wait. The port is so busy that it has two anchorages; an outer anchorage and an inner anchorage. Apparently, it's not uncommon for a ship to sit "on the hook" in the outer anchorage for a few days, then pick up anchor and re-anchor in the inner anchorage for a few more days, before finally being assigned dock space. So much for our three-day turnaround. And worse yet, it was clear I wasn't going to get to the pyramids anytime soon!

In the scheme of things, sitting at anchor, staring longingly at a port you know is going to be a lot of fun, is one of the worst emotional states anyone can feel. We ended up sitting at anchor for five days before we could get to the dock -- three days at the outer anchorage and two days at the inner anchorage. Man, were those days painful! Every day seemed to just creep along! For those five days, time seemed to stand still.

Well, everything in time, right? After all, if you're going get your ship together and stop just thinking about getting rich, and actually join the ranks of the 360° Wealthy, don't you think it's going to take some time? Well, yes, and no! I'll tell you why I say "yes" and "no" shortly.

Most of us tend to think of time in seconds, minutes, hours, days, weeks, and years. Depending on how old you are, you might be visualizing an analogue clock right now, with the seconds just ticking by.

In the western world, especially here in the U.S., you hear a lot about spending time, wasting time, making time, time standing still, and time flying by. If time is nothing more than a second hand ticking away, racking up minutes, hours, and days, how is it that sometimes it flies, and sometimes it seems to take forever?

"There were probably about five games in my career where everything was moving in slow motion and you could be out there all day, totally in the zone, and you don't even know where you are on the field, everything is just totally blocked out."

Lawrence Taylor was one of the best linebackers ever to play in the National Football League. I'll never forget his bone-crushing hit that ended Joe Theismann's career. But I digress. Taylor, like so many athletes who have been in "the zone," talks here about time slowing down. And in his case, it was a very welcome phenomenon.

How about the time you get together with an old high-school friend, one you haven't seen in several years? You get to talking and all of a sudden, you glance down at your watch and realize hours have passed, and you literally don't know where time went! You were enjoying the moment so completely that you lost all track of time.

In this case, time speeding up is a positive thing. You don't regret the time spent with your friend. You don't mourn the loss of those minutes and hours. Instead, you're grateful for the time spent.

In order to acquire 360° Wealth, you must have an appreciation for, and an understanding of, your relationship with time. Notice I didn't say "your relationship TO time," I said WITH time.

Just imagine being forced to stare at your favorite dessert from across the room and not being able to walk over and take a bite. Or gazing out the window at your brand-new car on a beautiful day, longing to take it for a drive and not being able to hop in and start it up.

If you were forced to carry on your normal day or routine and these obvious pleasures were right in front of you, but denied you until later, how would you feel? Do you think your day would just fly by or do you think the minutes would hang like hours? Of course, in these circumstances time would just creep along! And such was the case for me, trying to go about my day knowing how interesting and fun it would be if I could just get ashore to the pyramids.

Now let's flip it around. What would time feel like if you got in that brand-new car and took it for a leisurely drive, or took it out and hugged some curves on your favorite road? I'm guessing time would go by so quickly that you'd wonder where it went.

You (and I) have total control over our relationship WITH time. We can choose to think time is standing still, or time is flying by. The important thing is that it's really all in our mind.

This leads us, naturally, to our state of mind.

And what does our state of mind have to do with 360° Wealth?

EVERYTHING!

Henry Ford famously said, "Whether you think you can, or you think you can't – you're right."

Beliefs and faith are important, but your state of mind in any given moment is absolutely critical.

Your wealth is largely dependent on your state.

Your "state" is just another way for saying "how you feel." In the end all you're really after is a feeling.

Here's a brain twister for you…

We don't really want all the stuff and things we think wealth will bring, we just think we do. When I say I want to fly to my Hawaiian vacation on my private jet, all I really, really want is the feeling I believe I will get when I fly private.

Now here's the unique twist (like so many unique twists we've seen along this journey).

If I can put myself into a state that "feels" exactly how I'll feel when I'm on my private jet, then making the jet appear in my life becomes a possibility that can become "real" for me.

Here's the great news ....

You can put yourself into an incredible state instantly. You already "manipulate" and/or change your state several times a day, and you probably don't even realize it! Think about it, when you first get up in the morning, if part of your routine is to look into the mirror, you are instantly putting yourself into a certain state. When you look in the mirror on any given day what's staring back at you may make you feel tired, less than pretty or handsome, and un-energized. On the other hand, on a different day, you might feel energized, eager to conquer the day, and invincible. Those are two different days and two extremes, and you can feel those or anything in between. You've just put yourself into a state.

If you're a "first thing in the morning mirror person," think about how the rest of the day goes when you create the tired, unenergized state. I'll bet you trip over a toy on your way to the kitchen, fumble with the coffee maker and the traffic seems extra heavy on your way to work.

Conversely, how does your day seem to go when you start out in the eager to conquer the day? I'll bet things seem to go smoothly, the coffee tastes extra good for some reason, the drive to work is pleasant and you find the perfect parking spot when you get there.

Recently, I was asked to be on a panel of entrepreneurs at a large gathering of solopreneurs and small business owners, about 500 business owners who had come to Denver for a three-day conference on building and growing their businesses.

Our panel was scheduled to go on stage around 3:00 p.m. of the second day. The first day and a half of the conference had been outstanding; my friend, mentor, and business partner Rachael Jayne Groover and her business partner/husband Datta had done a masterful job of giving the participants tremendous value - so no pressure on us (the panel), right? Wrong!

I knew, and I'm sure my fellow panel members did too, that we needed to knock it out of the park, so we could keep the excellent momentum of the conference going. Now, that would be a lot of pressure for a mere mortal, but not for someone who understands "state," and how to create an aligned feeling.

As I'm sitting in the audience, along with my fellow panelists, I'm actively putting myself into a great, powerful, "value-giving" state. I'm doing this by playing, in my mind, one of my favorite inspirational songs. With each guitar chord and drum beat I'm getting more and more inspired, and at the same time feeling calm and focused. By the time we're introduced and called up on stage, I'm totally relaxed, focused, and at the same time, energized to deliver outstanding value in a clear, concise, and powerful way.

So we all walk up on stage to this incredible, thunderous applause

> **Here's another clue to add to your clue-box...**
> **State precedes reality!**

I want to introduce you to a concept I call "Future-stating."

Future-stating is the act of putting yourself into a vibrational state that is a match to the vibrational state you will be in when that which you want appears.

The interesting thing here, and the key to remember, is that it doesn't matter how, or what, causes you to get into your future-state. What's most important is that you get into a vibrational match with what you want in the future.

Let me give you an example ....

Let's say you want to travel to your next business or pleasure trip by private jet. As you already know, your jet has already been created and it's just waiting for you to "see" it. So how do you go about "seeing" it and having it become a part of Your World? You "Future-State!"

How will you feel as you climb the steps to your private jet? How will you feel as you sit in the rich leather, overstuffed, fully reclining, cabin seat? How will you feel as the pilot asks if you're ready to leave, because the flight departure and destination are completely up to you? How will you feel when the flight attendant asks what you would like prepared for lunch and points you to a fully stocked bar and an elegant platter of Hors d'oeuvres? Feeling these feelings is what I call Future-Stating.

Do you have an idea of what that would feel like? By the way, if flying around on your private jet is not your thing, pick something that is. Do it now, so you can better experience what I mean by Future-Stating.

Got the feeling? Good.

At this point you might be thinking, "I want a private jet (or something else 'big'), but right now it's so far out of my belief of what's possible that I can't sustain the feeling of having it."

Or for you it might be a case of wanting this future thing but your self-talk is so strong that you can't stay in the future-state.

No worries – because this is what's really cool about the relationship of your state to your ability to create 360° Wealth. Check this out, it's super cool and super important.

To "see" your private jet, or whatever you've decided you want, you don't even have to think about the jet! As soon as you've stated your desire to have something, it's possible for you to have it because it already exists. To see it as a real and tangible part of Your World, all you have to do, after stating that you want it, is to put yourself into a state that is a vibrational match to that which you want.

For example, you've decided to buy a new car in the next few months, and that really excites you. If the feeling you'll have when you drive off the lot in your new car happens to be a vibrational match to the feeling you would have flying around in your private jet, then you're all set. All you need to do is maintain the vibrational state of "new-car-dom" and I promise you, you will eventually see the jet as well. I know it sounds freaky, but believe me, this is the way it all works.

Yes, indeed, "state" is super important to creating a world that looks the way you want it to look.

Here's another reason why state is so important. Depending on your state, you will be either dragged through your day or propelled effortlessly through it.

There's no doubt about it, we live in a world of constant and seemingly unending information bombardment. To me, the information that is constantly coming at me reminds me of that scene in *The Matrix* where the bullets are flying at Neo. If we're not ready for it, or we aren't in a good vibrational state, those "information bullets" will do normal bullet damage!

On the other hand, if our state is amped up and we are in a great vibrational situation, we can handle those "information bullets" just like Neo did. When you put yourself into a great state, things seem to come at you in slow motion just like they did for Lawrence Taylor. You feel as though you have more than enough time to react, and even pro-act. You can pick and choose the information you want to let in and use. This is all so important in the realm of 360° Wealth.

There are a number of ways to deliberately put yourself into a certain state. I'm going to give you a few that work really well for me and that I use all the time. As with everything you read in this book, these aren't the only ways or absolutes. You need to figure out what works for you.

- Movement
- Posture
- Your facial expressions
- Music
- Change of environment
- All of the above, or any combination of the above.

Now I feel compelled to also mention that you can change your state in other ways, which in my opinion are ultimately destructive, therefore I don't personally recommend them. Here's my list of ways to change your state that I DON'T recommend:

- Drugs
- Alcohol
- Food

But hey, you're a grownup, right? So you choose what works for you.

Let's dive a little deeper, then let's see if we can find John Morris and own and operate some ships!

I remember a night, probably before Jackie (my wife) and I were even dating. I was having dinner with good friends, at this cool little bar/restaurant in Solana Beach near San Diego. I don't see them much now, but Sandy and Alan were empty nesters back then, which was perfect when I was single because our lifestyles were much more similar. But Jackie and I have been raising kids for the last 20 years, so I don't get a chance to spend time with them much anymore. It's a shame because they are both brilliant in their own ways, and a lot of fun.

That night we had just been served our cocktails when the conversation somehow shifted to energy and matter. Alan proclaimed something I had never heard of before. He went on to tell me that nothing in our world is solid and that everything is just energy. And Sandy chimed in to say that what makes something appear solid is our attention to it.

This conversation blew me away, because although the three of us had had many interesting, provocative, and even controversial conversations, this one seemed actually unreal. I remember saying to them, incredulously, "You mean to tell me that this table we're sitting at isn't real?" I remember gently pounding my fist on the table as I'm saying this, wondering how that table could be energy and not solid matter. That conversation, almost 30 years ago, stayed with me. But it wasn't until years later I would realize how what we talked about that night was so profound.

Watching the movie, *What the Bleep*, it all began to make sense. I highly recommend you watch it, too. I first saw it 20 years after that dinner conversation with Sandy and Alan (I told you they were brilliant!). The movie format provides the visual input combined with language, which makes deep comprehension easier.

So here's my take on that wisdom. The first realization is that everything you can see, touch, feel, is brought about by your attention to it. Yes, you can see, feel, and touch the dining table. But imagine for a moment if your consciousness decided there was no table, or could not conceive the possibility that there is a table. Would you still see the table? Probably not. But that is almost impossible to consider, because we tend to believe that everything already exists before we experience it, rather than considering it exists because we allow the possibility.

Now this isn't a book about quantum physics so that's really all I'm gonna say about it. If you want to dive deeper there are lots of great resources, but we're focused on getting your shit (oh sorry, I mean SHIP) together!

So let's get back to finding John Morris, my heretofore "mythical" future partner.

So here's exactly what I did...

I started to think about, and envision my life, owning and operating ships. I created in my mind's eye the perfect picture of my new partner, John Morris. I pictured, in great detail, the two of us traveling the world looking for ships. I pictured, in great detail, the two of us sitting in corporate boardrooms and in high-powered bankers' offices negotiating finance deals and ship deals. I felt exactly how it would feel to climb the gangway of ships that we owned and talk with the captains and crews we employed. And, I pictured myself in my office running the day-to-day shipping operations of our maritime empire.

I envisioned all this (and more) in great detail every day for several months. Yes, months! But you know what? The time seemed to fly by. I was having so much fun thinking about, and then acting on, my most desired outcome that it seemed like in no time I had results.

And what exactly was the result?

Well, The Call, of course!

Yeah, I think you've gotten enough of the back story to appreciate The Call like I did. I think I've just about given you all you need to appreciate how creating wealth in a 360° way works. We have one more blade of the Wealth propeller to cover, but I think that can wait just a little bit longer.

Okay, but there is just one more piece of the puzzle that I need to tell you about before I circle back to the beginning of my story. Are you ready? I think you are! Let me tell you about another really interesting book.

15

"I'd Tell Atlas To Shrug!"

Fransisco D' Anconia: "If you saw Atlas, the giant who holds the world on his shoulders, if you saw that he stood, blood running down his chest, his knees buckling, his arms trembling but still trying to hold the world aloft with the last of his strength, and the greater his effort the heavier the world bore down upon his shoulders -- What would you tell him?"

Hank Rearden: "I ... don't know. What ... could he do? What would YOU tell him?"

Fransisco D' Anconia: "To shrug."

(Passage from *Atlas Shrugged* by Ayn Rand)

Atlas Shrugged, by Ayn Rand is one of my all-time favorite books. I think it leaves a lot of clues about wealth, the 360° way. While the book is not specifically about wealth as I'm describing it here, it does present some very interesting concepts about what True Wealth is.

Written in 1957, but set sometime in the future, the book portrays Rand's point of view that all the smart, creative "doers" like the artists, scholars, engineers, and industrialists are carrying the weight of the world on their shoulders, just like Atlas is depicted as doing. In Rand's vision of the future these "doers" are all misunderstood, mistreated, and adversely effected by the policies of their government. So, they all go on strike and basically "shrug" off the weight of the world, by disappearing from their businesses and occupations and leaving the rest of the world to fend for itself.

The person who has organized and coordinated this "doers" strike is a brilliant but disgruntled factory engineer named John Galt. Although Rand doesn't tell us much about John Galt until the very end of the book -- in fact we don't even know the name of this mysterious factory worker until at least two-thirds of the way through the book -- the phrase "who is John Galt" seems to be on the tip of everyone's tongue whenever they are frustrated or can't explain why something has happened.

Toward the end of the book John Galt reveals himself to the world and explains why he has organized all the world's business leaders, artists, scientists, engineers, and scholars (aka "the doers") and convinced them to go on strike and disappear. He goes public by hijacking a powerful radio station and delivering his manifesto to the world.

Imagine a world that has spiraled into chaos because all its leaders have gone on strike. Then imagine how that world would react if all of the sudden a voice came over the radio and simultaneously announced to everyone in the world what has happened and why. This was the exact situation at the climax of *Atlas Shrugged.*

Toward the end of the book there is a moment when John Galt announces to the world that the "doers" are no longer going to support the weight of the world on their shoulders. He begins his interruptive, surprise, unexpected, "tell all" manifesto by first announcing "This is John Galt!"

I remember vividly, the first time I read the book how those four words – "This is John Galt" -- totally knocked me off my feet. Throughout the book Ayn Rand had fed me bits and pieces of John Galt's philosophy and his genius; first without even mentioning his name or connecting this philosophy to a specific person. Then, over time, she took me on a journey to discover who this mystery person is, why he had decided to organize the world's economic and thought leaders and convince them to abandon their businesses and careers and disappear, and exactly how he did it.

Those four words knocked me off my feet because throughout the book I became more and more absorbed in, and enamored with, the lives and the accomplishments of the "doers." These were men and women who lead what I would characterize as 360° Wealthy lives. They all definitely had their "ships together!" They were using all the support tools of our ship's wheel and they were using at least five of the blades of our Wealth propeller to propel themselves forward.

And then there was this mysterious guy who recognized the 360° Wealth they had created not only for themselves, but for the world at large. I wanted desperately to know who the mystery man was. As I got deeper and deeper into the book I had an inkling that our mystery man might be John Galt, but I wasn't 100% sure until I heard him introduce himself with those four powerfully stated words – "This is John Galt!"

As I said earlier, it's funny how certain things can happen to you seemingly out of the blue, and in hindsight, or much later, you see how profound they were. I told you two such things happened to me; they were years apart from each other but both so profound. You already know about movies talking directly to me. Well, the other instance is...

The Call.

16

The Call

WARNING! If you read the first chapter or two, got super curious about The Call, then skipped ahead to this chapter … STOP, put the book down, give yourself 40 lashes, then walk the plank, because you've just committed a "major book crime." You should report to Captain's Mast, plead guilty and suffer the consequences!

Perhaps even more importantly, you've cheated yourself out of most of the detail you need to get your ship together and stop just thinking about getting rich! You want True 360° Wealth? Well then flip back the pages and take it all in. There's gold there, I promise.

Okay, I'm off the soapbox. Let's re-set the scene.

There I was, sitting at my desk, in a small unassuming office, staring out my window with the awe-inspiring view of a parking lot. I'm trying to keep myself awake and at the same time trying to look busy, even though no one was looking over my shoulder, and I didn't need to look busy for anyone in particular.

We were a super small company – I think there were only about six of us, from the president on down to the receptionist. The company was only a couple of years old and was started by a couple of fellow Kings Pointers who had graduated a few years before me.

Admiralty Systems (the name of the company), was affectionately known in the Washington, DC area as a "Beltway Bandit." In other words, we were one of several government contractors constantly trolling the Commerce Business Daily publication looking for federal government contracts on which we could bid. Yes, and while we didn't actually do it, we were a business just like those guys that were selling the federal government $8,000 toilet seats. Hey, if we could have gotten in on that racket maybe I wouldn't have written this book!

Admiralty Systems was an engineering consulting firm that specialized in providing services to the government. Consulting firm Beltway Bandits basically bid and won contracts based on the strength of the resumes of their owners and employees. Tom and Guy, the two majority partners who started the firm, needed some additional marine engineering "expertise" (aka a good resume) to bid on and have a chance to win a particular contract. I had worked with Tom at another Beltway Bandit, ROH, Inc., so he knew me, and when he found out my brother Brian and I had closed our restaurant, he asked if I wanted to join them and "lend" Admiralty Systems my resume.

The decision was a quick and easy one. These types of decisions tend to be a lot quicker and easier when you're broke, in debt, and negotiating with the IRS on back sales taxes. Not to mention that my last "job" had literally brought me to tears!

Before I even started at Admiralty I told Tom and Guy what I wanted to do. I told them about my desired outcome to own and operate ships and my quest to find the mysterious, and somewhat elusive, John Morris. To their credit and integrity, they couldn't have been more supportive. Our working relationship was pretty simple and straight forward – as long as I did what needed to be done to bid on, win, and maintain our government contracts, I could do whatever else I needed to do in pursuit of my ship-owning/operating outcome.

I worked there for a little less than a year. I think it's kind of a tell-tale sign of my overall mindset and my affinity for the work, that I can't really remember what I worked on while I was there. All I know is that it was marine-engineering related, and boring as hell – no offense to Tom and Guy!

Over the course of these pages in this book you and I have traveled through several time periods, related to many different maritime personalities, and metaphorically traveled the seven seas. Allow me to anchor you to the Admiralty Systems (pre The Call) timeframe.

Beezer's (our restaurant) had been "temporarily" closed for over a year now, and I had officially gotten under way on my dream of owning ships. I think you could say I was making way -- but not very rapidly. By this time I had sailed on my U.S. Coast Guard license for several years and I had upgraded my license to Second Assistant Engineer. I had been studying maritime business by reading anything I could get my hands on, and I had been pounding the pavement and talking to anyone who would listen to what I wanted to do. I was almost universally praised for my insight regarding the value of partnering with someone with experience in the areas where I lacked experience or expertise, and the one name that kept surfacing time and again was John Morris. But just as quickly as the name was mentioned, it was always followed by something like, "But I don't know how to get hold of him."

So there I was, one bitter cold winter's day, sitting at my desk, bored out of my mind, listening to my co-workers brag and bitch about meaningless trivialities. Although I don't remember specifically, I was probably either thinking about what I wanted for lunch that day, why the Washington Redskins hadn't won more Super Bowls, or what my next move should be in pursuit of John Morris and my outcome. And then it happened ....

The intercom on my desk squawked and the voice of our receptionist/office manager Tina came blasting through and jarred me from my innocuous thoughts. Her words, although quite simple, will forever mark for me the beginning of a true transformation in thought, actions, and results. All she said was, "Del, you have a call on line one."

I certainly wasn't expecting a call from anyone. It was mid-week so I wasn't planning anything social with any friends that might have necessitated a call. I had touched base with all my family recently, so a call from a family member wasn't expected, and calls related to what I was currently working on were few and far between. So, I think it was with equal parts disinterest and curiosity that I punched the button for line one and said, "Del Lewis."

What I heard next almost knocked me out of my desk chair. Not an easy feat, considering my legs were tucked under my desk and the arms of my chair were pressed against the desk, securely "locking" me in.

The voice on the other end of the phone was a deep baritone, very articulate, but with an ever so slight froggy tone suggesting to me that he was from an older generation. He started the conversation with just five simple words – "Del, this is John Morris."

Have you ever had one of those moments that you know in reality only lasts a second or two but in that short spurt of time, days, months, or even years seem to flash before your eyes? Well in that instant, what flashed before me was all the work, effort, trials, tribulations, persistence, phone calls, meetings, dead-ends, excitement, joys, setbacks, and progress I'd made over the past year diligently trying to find this mystery man named John Morris. And all of the sudden, there he was, on the other end of my telephone line. It was truly my "John Galt" moment.

Imagine a person's life that is turned somewhat upside down because they've had both the good fortune, and the misfortune, of determining that what they were doing wasn't working for them. And as they begin to get their shit together and build their metaphoric ship they know that a key piece of the puzzle is missing. They think they know what that missing piece is, but they're not 100% sure it even exists. Then imagine how that person would react if all of the sudden a voice came over the telephone and announced: "I'm here!" "I exist," "And in fact I've been looking for you!," "You're the missing piece to MY puzzle!" This was exactly what occurred at the apex of my quest to manifest my outcome. And this is what 360° Wealth looks and feels like. That was the day I got The Call.

So almost 500 years after Columbus set sail, got lost, and eventually discovered The New World, I had started a journey of my own. No, I didn't find any new real estate, enslave a native population, or plunder for gold and spices. But I did get lost for a short period of time, and then eventually discover a New World; one inhabited by the 360° Wealthy.

On that journey I figured out that the biggest difference between the 360° Wealthy and everybody else is that the 360° Wealthy have figured out how to propel and steer toward their wealth, and they do it in a complete, 360° sort of way. Here are the visuals of that process once again for your information.

You, too, can use this model to get your ship together. It all starts with an awareness of what you want. Then learning how to navigate. Next you plot your course, being aware that you'll probably need to course-correct. Find and recruit your crew, understanding that you are a member of several tribes or crews already. All of this is for the benefit and manifestation of the fifth propeller blade, your most desired outcome. And remember, throughout the voyage you'll steer toward your wealth by effectively using time, money, health, relationships, thoughts (or imagination), and things.

But what about the sixth propeller blade in our model?

Well, I guess you'll have to navigate over to the next page to find out. It's a biggie and it makes your pursuing 360° Wealth today so much easier than it ever has been.

See you at the next port of call (that's more maritime-speak for "turn the f_ _ _ _ ing page!") ☺

17

The Sixth Propeller Blade

On December 25th, many years ago and thousands of miles away from the United States, a child was born. Some would look at this child as a savior, others would proclaim this birth as perhaps the most significant event in our world to date. Still others would have varying degrees of interaction, acceptance, and belief.

Regardless of where you live today, or whether you are a Christian, Jew, Muslim, Atheist, Agnostic, or something in between, there is no question that this birth changed the world.

Of course, I'm referring to the invention of the World Wide Web!

Located in western Switzerland, not far from the French border where the Rhône exits Lake Geneva, sits the small town of Meyrin, population less than 200,000, and the home of CERN. CERN stands for European Organization for Nuclear Research (actually the acronym is from the French translation: Conseil Européene pour la Recherche Nucléaire).

Forget about the acronym, though. What's most important about CERN is that it's the birthplace of the World Wide Web. Yes, on a crisp, clear Christmas morn, Tim Berners-Lee (not Al Gore, by the way) typed a few keys on his computer in Switzerland, accessed some information on a computer half way around the world, and the internet was born!

The World Wide Web and the internet, just like everything else in our world, started as a simple thought – the perfect illustration of the overall 360° Wealth model I've been outlining here.

Literally one man had a thought -- an idea -- that became an outcome with profound impact, not only on his world but the world at large. This child of an idea, once birthed, was adopted and adapted by countless others and grew into the internet.

Think of all the different crews who use the internet today, of all the crews the internet has spawned, and all the new crews you are now able to become a part of because one person deliberately set a course and navigated toward an outcome.

Here's how it happened. In the 1980s hundreds of scientists from around the world travelled to CERN to do their nuclear research experiments. At that time, Tim

Berners-Lee was a software consultant at CERN and in charge of helping the scientists connect to CERN's mainframe computer. The scientists would bring their own computers and "plug in" to the CERN mainframe, do their research work, "unplug," and go back home. The scientists connected to the mainframe using a computer language Tim had created for that purpose.

Getting all these disparate computers to talk to the CERN mainframe was no small feat, but Tim made it happen. Then Tim thought it would be even cooler if all the computers could share their research and information with each other even after the scientists returned to their home labs.

Tim had an idea that research and discovery could be greatly enhanced if the scientists could go from having a "one-to-one" connection (individual scientist computer to mainframe) into a "many-to-many" communication (scientist to mainframe and scientist to scientist). So, he invented "http," a way for a scientist to find a document; "URL," an address where the document was located; and "html," a language so all this could work.

Imagine how different our lives would be today without the invention of the internet.

Some 25 years after the birth of the internet I sat in my house having a conversation with my parents. Both my parents are University of Kansas (KU) alums. In fact, I have several aunts, uncles, cousins, two grandparents, and at least one great-grandparent who are KU alums. As a result, we're major KU basketball fans. Anyway, on this particular night we were trying to remember how many NCAA national championships KU had won in basketball.

After a few minutes of deliberation, I got up from the couch, walked into the next room and returned with a shiny object about the size of a piece of printer paper and weighing no more than two pounds. I pressed a few plastic buttons and told my parents with 100% certainty (at least in my mind) that KU had been to 14 Final Four's and had won the national championship no fewer than three times!

Thank you, Tim Berners-Lee!

Tim Berners-Lee, is not a "maritime guy" but just like all the other incredible people we've seen in the chapters of this book, he is no different, better, or smarter than you. In fact, the only thing each has done (in their own unique way) is use some form of the system I outlined for you.

In my wealth model the sixth propeller blade is kind of a wild card. Throughout history there is usually one key aspect, innovation, or trend we can find that fundamentally changes the way we do things, and in our present day 360° Wealth model it's the internet. If we were using our model back in the late 1700s our 6th blade might have been the industrial revolution. In the late 1800s it probably would have been the telephone because it fundamentally changed the way we live.

If we had been living in the early 1900s and employing our 360° Wealth model, the sixth blade innovation would have most certainly been flight. Being a maritime guy I can't help but point out the parallels between the aviation industry and the shipping industry. Many people don't realize the fact that the dawn of commercial air travel was at the height of commercial ship travel. And since I'm all about your shit (ah, I mean your "ship") I thought I'd point out the parallels.

Ever notice that your plane arrives and departs from the air "port?" And in fact, even before airports, planes took off and landed on the water. Don't just believe me, check out some of the old (original) advertisements for Pan Am airlines. Also, in the beginning planes were actually called "air ships."

The term "pilot" is actually a maritime term, and the pilot is a member of the plane's "crew." One of the first people you see when "boarding" a plane is now called by the politically correct title of "flight attendant", but they used to be called "stewards" and "stewardesses" because they were members of the Steward's Department and their job was to take care of the passenger's every need. Man, I wish those golden days of in-flight customer service would return!

Finally, I think it's interesting to note the various classes of service aboard a plane, and the different "cabins" on a plane. The "First Class Cabin," "Business Class Cabin," and what used to be called "Tourist Class Cabin" (now most often referred to as "Coach Class"), are directly related to the classes of service aboard the classic ocean liners of their day. I even find it interesting to note that the proverbial lowest of the low class on a plane – those coach passengers relegated to the back of the plane near the engines, are just like those poor peasants who travelled in "Steerage Class" in the bowels of the ship near the engines, shaft, and propeller.

You see, so much of our would can be tied back to humanity's rich maritime culture. Just another great reason to Get Your Ship Together and stop just thinking about growing rich!

So there you have it, all six blades of our 360° Wealth Propeller. Here's the complete graphic ....

Now let me show you what it all looks like when in action ....

18

All For One And One For All

Your 360° Wealth propeller has been constructed and it's ready for you to use to propel you to Total Wealth. Let me show you what it looks like when it all comes together.

Shortly after I got "The Call" I had "The Meeting." Yes, John Morris really did exist! He really was an entrepreneur, and he was in the shipping business! Well, actually he wasn't "in" the shipping business just yet, but he wanted to be, and that was even better for me because he was looking for a crew to help him get to his "most desired port of call" (aka his outcome).

I think it was only a day or two after we talked on The Call that we met in person. John happened to be in town for a meeting with Bill Charrier, the Founder and CEO of American Automar, a company that specialized in buying foreign flag ships, reflagging them under the U.S. flag and chartering (if you recall, that's the maritime term for "renting") them to the federal government. American

Automar's office was in Georgetown, so John and I agreed to meet for lunch there. In hindsight I think there was a certain degree of serendipity that we decided to meet in Georgetown.

For those of you who have never been to Washington, DC, or Georgetown for that matter, here's a quick geography/history lesson ... I think you'll agree; the choice of venue just seems right.

Georgetown is a historic neighborhood located in the northwest quadrant of Washington, DC. Its narrow streets (some still cobblestone) are lined with colonial style town homes, many of which were built in the late 1700s. Today Georgetown is an urban mix of residential, commercial, bars, dining, and entertainment establishments. Its two main streets, Wisconsin Avenue and M street, are usually hopping until the early morning hours almost every night.

Situated along the Potomac River, the area now known as Georgetown was founded in 1751 and was originally a part of the colony of Maryland. There was a certain serendipity in meeting John Morris there because way before Georgetown was the playground of yuppie "DINKS" (people with "Dual Incomes and No Kids") and spoiled Georgetown University students, it was a working port. Multi-masted sailing ships brought goods from other parts of the eastern seaboard up the Potomac to what is now Washington, DC., and on one infamous day in the fall of 1838, a ship loaded with 272 slaves – African-American men, women and children – set sail from the port of Georgetown, destined for the plantations of the deep south. The irony of ironies was that these people (yes, they were "people") were the "property" of the Jesuit priests who ran Georgetown University; at the time the country's premier Catholic university. That fall day in 1838, 272 people set sail for what I'm sure was a very unpleasant future.

Conversely, the day John and I met in Georgetown we were two "totally free" African American men metaphorically setting sail on a voyage to create a new breed of shipping company, and I find it interesting that we chose to do so not far from the same shores that at one time traded men, women, and children as property and was simultaneously the birthplace of a new nation and a type of government that would ultimately (albeit slowly) give John and me the opportunity of a lifetime.

As if this whole journey from weeping uncontrollably in my own restaurant to figuring out my most desired outcome, to searching for this guy named John Morris, to finally sitting down with him, weren't bizarre and crazy (good) enough, the first words out of John's mouth were

"I'm so glad I found you! I've been looking for you for quite a while!"

He had been looking for me? That totally blew me away.

Actually, knowing what I know now, I realize this is a perfect illustration of the way 360° Wealth works. When you put the blades of the Wealth Propeller in motion, the things that you need to make your desired outcomes become reality are automatically attracted to you. Amazingly, exactly what you need gets sucked into your propeller; and at the perfect time. If you've ever seen a video or photos of a propeller doing its work in the deep blue ocean then you know just what a powerful tool it is!

While it wasn't until much later in my business career that I would be able to articulate my state of being at the time of The Meeting, I can say now without a doubt that I was wealthy in a 360° way. And it is my firm belief that having The Meeting was a direct result of being in a state of 360° wealth. I can now look back and note that at that exact time I had all the elements of the Ship's Wheel I outlined earlier.

I had TIME – Because I was working at a stress-free, unchallenging job, I had time to pursue my most desired outcome of owning and operating ships, and I had the time to help John build the foundation of our new company.

I had MONEY – Yes, even for a serial entrepreneur such as me, I gotta say, making money from a job can have its benefits! With my salary from Admiralty Systems I was able to pay my bills and meet the obligations I had outstanding from my restaurant venture. Money oftentimes gets a bum rap; you know, all that stuff about it not buying you love or happiness, or he love of it being the root of all evil, etc. But I gotta tell ya, I've had times in my life when the amount of money I had was sufficient, and times when it was real tight, and I'll take money over no money every time! Yeah, I know, I've said over and over again throughout this book that wealth is not just about money, and it's not, but it is an equally important part of the equation. I owe a lot to Tom and Guy, and the other founders of Admiralty Systems, for thinking enough of my background and experience to allow me to work there. Thanks, guys! Bottom line: being able to pay my bills and feed myself allowed me the freedom of thought and freedom from stress to propel toward Total (360°) Wealth.

I had my HEALTH – I was working out five times a week, swimming, running, playing basketball, and lifting weights. I was eating well (still drinking a few beers on the weekend – full disclosure), and I felt great and on top of my game.

I had great RELATIONSHIPS – I have always been fortunate to have outstanding family relationships. As I have grown older, my family has grown with the addition of spouses, kids, nieces and nephews, and at the core, my relationship with my mom, dad, and three brothers has always been super-good and super-strong. We've always loved and cared for each other and had each other's back, regardless of the situation. And like any family, we've had our share of shitty situations, stress, and strain. I don't ever take my family lightly or for granted. I know that not everyone has a rock-solid nuclear family in their corner. But I did, and do. At the time I met John I wasn't married, and I don't believe I was dating anyone in particular, but I was in a great place with regard to friend and family relationships. Being in a good "relationship place" is critical to becoming 360° Wealthy.

My THOUGHTS were positive, energizing, and inspiring – and everything starts with a thought! And while there's a hell of lot more that's required for True Wealth, you'll never get there unless your thoughts are aligned. From the moment I had started my quest to own and operate ships I had put myself into an energized and inspiring future-state. Of course I wasn't in this state 100% of the time but I was in this future-state the majority of the time. And when I was really in vibrational alignment with how I would feel when I got what I wanted I could feel, taste, smell, and hear what things would be like when I had realized my most desired outcome. This is powerful stuff, and completely within your control.

I had lots of THINGS at my disposal. Recognizing the things (or tools) you have at your disposal is a key to harnessing your True Wealth. On my voyage in pursuit of my outcome I had access to great communication tools. I had access to express mail service, simple, cost effective, long distance phone service, I could travel at will, and I had great office resources. These things may sound primitive to many of you, but you have to remember, when we started our company the internet was still just a thought in Tim Berners-Lee's head.

Over lunch that day John laid out for me, in great detail, exactly what he wanted to accomplish. He told me about his amazing journey and gave me some enticing snippets of his background. He had a law degree and had practiced law in a prestigious Chicago law firm. It was there that he was first exposed to the maritime industry and the business of shipping.

One day, one of his partners dropped a file on his desk involving a client of the firm who was involved in a legal dispute over the fees from a PL480 cargo. And at that point you could say John's voyage got under way!

Public Law 480 (PL480), officially called The Agricultural Trade Development Assistance Act of 1954, but more commonly referred to as just PL480 or the "Food for Peace Program" is a federal law signed into effect by President Eisenhower.

According to President Eisenhower, the purpose of the program was to "lay the basis for a permanent expansion of our exports of agricultural products with lasting benefits to ourselves and peoples of other lands."

In a nutshell, it was a way for the U.S. to share our excess farm production with the rest of the world. Ike believed this program would have the dual benefit of helping starving and famine-stricken nations while bolstering our philanthropic and diplomatic image in the eyes of the world. The program was, and still is, managed through, and administered by, three different agencies; the U.S. Agency for International Development (USAID or just AID), the Department of State, and the Department of Agriculture.

Since its inception, the PL 480 Program has benefitted more than three billion people in more than 150 countries. In fact, the United States currently provides approximately 60 percent of the world's food aid.

The U.S.-grown and processed agricultural commodities that are delivered around the world are shipped primarily on U.S.-flagged ships. At one point the law was amended to stipulate that at least 75% of all Food for Peace cargos be shipped on U.S.-flagged ships.

As John is telling me all this I could see the sparkle in his eyes and the intensity in his facial features. I could tell he was building to a very important point; something that he was tremendously excited about. He went on to tell me that his client had chartered a U.S. flag ship, then submitted a bid to the USAID, won the bid, and then delivered a Food for Peace cargo to Karachi, Pakistan. And then John said, "That's when the shit hit the fan!"

Turns out, because of certain intricacies within the deal, John's client didn't get paid the hundreds of thousands of dollars he was entitled to for setting up the deal, chartering the ship, and delivering the cargo.

Long story short, John got his client all the money he was owed, but for John the hidden gem in the whole ordeal was what he learned about the contractual and financial aspects of the maritime industry; and, specifically, how lucrative it could be to do business with our federal government.

It was obvious John had a lot more he wanted to share with me. He had this unique way of expressing tremendous energy and passion with a simple smile, a slight raising of one eyebrow, and a quick tussle of his thick, curly, salt-and-pepper head of hair. And I gotta tell ya, John's passion was contagious!

He goes on to tell me that in preparing to argue his client's case he not only learned the profitable economics of the U.S PL480 trade and how a certain percentage of that trade had to be delivered on U.S. flag ships, he also learned about contract set-asides.

He said, "Del when I learned the ins and outs of the PL480 trade all I wanted to do was charter me a ship and deliver a cargo. I figured I could clear three to four hundred thousand dollars easy. I figured I'd do that once or twice and then ride off into the sunset. Hell, I didn't need to be full time in this thing. I was pretty much financially set already. I'm retired from the full-time practice of law. I've been teaching law for several years now, and I helped build the law school at ASU (Arizona State University). I'm a tenured professor there, and I love it. So life is good!"

Then he went on: "But when I found out about DOD (Department of Defense) contracts and their mandatory set asides my thinking completely changed and I decided I wanted to go into the shipping business big time! Del, I want to be the first minority-owned company to win a shipping contract with the Department of Defense and the Military Sealift Command. And I need a maritime guy to help me do that. And I want YOU to be that guy!"

Then, just like in the Pretty Woman movie scene I described earlier, John said, "Mr. Lewis, you and I are going to operate ships together, great big ships!"

And to paraphrase a line from another popular movie, Jerry Maguire, I can tell you now, "He had me at 'Mr. Lewis'!"

I was all in and couldn't wait to start our voyage!

John had uncovered a niche within the maritime industry that had yet to be successfully taken advantage of. Government contract set asides for "small disadvantaged" businesses had been around since the 1940s. They were first created to help smaller companies get federal government contracts so that they could help with the war effort. The basic premise of a "small disadvantaged set-aside" was that certain government contracts, specifically Department of Defense contracts, would be "set aside" for small businesses. In other words the big boys couldn't bid on them. This worked so well for the federal government during World War II and the Korean War that when the Small Business Administration (SBA) became a permanent government agency in 1958, small business set-asides became a permanent peace-time practice as well. When Congress passed the Small Business Act of 1958, transforming the SBA into a permanent agency, the mandate and authority to set aside certain contracts for small disadvantaged businesses was included in Section 8(a) of the act. Nowadays these government set asides are often referred to as "8(a) Set Asides."

Of course, true to our country's brilliant history, it took us a long time to realize that "small and disadvantaged" could also include "minority owned and operated." So, in actuality, from its inception in 1941 until the late '70s, the concept of small disadvantaged business set asides really should have been called "small disadvantaged (WHITE MALE) business set asides"! But the Feds eventually got it right and started to mandate that 8(a) set asides be focused on minority- and women-owned and operated businesses, and through an executive order in 1978, these DOD contract set asides started to truly benefit those who needed the competitive help the most. But until John Morris came along no one had taken advantage of these set asides in the maritime industry.

One of the things I loved and respected the most about John was that he knew what he didn't know! And he never let his lack of knowledge set him back. In fact he used his lack of certain knowledge to propel him forward by seeking the answers to the things he didn't know. This is a key trait of the 360° Wealthy.

As you assemble the six blades of your Wealth Propeller, you always want to be aware of what's missing and what you don't know. After all, if you don't know that you don't know something, how will you ever realize you need it? Now that's a mouthful (I know), but dissect it and take it to heart. It'll pay dividends, I promise!

Pop quiz – what's the Fourth Wealth Propeller blade?

Yep, it's your Crew (also might be called your team or your tribe).

As John and I were finishing lunch that day in Georgetown he told me about the crew he was assembling. He said that the core of our crew would be him, his son John, Jr., and me (should I decide to accept the mission he was laying before me). He told me he had already created a company called Red River Shipping and the three of us would be the sole owners.

Over time John Sr., JJ, and I became a lot like the Three Musketeers. We each had a talent and a certain experience that would propel our business forward. John Sr. was the visionary and the elder statesman. He was our chief negotiator and our financier. John Jr. was the business brains of our operation. He was a genius at business operations and administration, and he kept us on track financially. And I had the maritime experience. Of the three of us, I think I was the only one who had ever actually been on a cargo ship. As we mariners like to say, I was the only one who knew that the "pointy" end of the ship was the bow!

Even though our talents and experience were extensive, John knew what we didn't know. John knew that we didn't know how to own and operate ships. And we didn't know how to successfully bid on Department of Defense (DOD) and Military Sealift Command (MSC) contracts.

In a stroke of genius John figured out a way to get us the ship ownership and operation expertise we lacked while at the same time allowing us to maintain control over our business and build it the way we wanted to. The way John negotiated the structure of our business going forward not only helped us to learn the ropes and successfully grow, but it also fully complied with the letter of the 8(a) Set Aside law. The intent of the law was to help those minority, and women-owned, small, disadvantaged businesses to better compete with the big boys, and the underlying intention was to help those businesses that were truly owned and operated by minorities and women. But as is the case in most special circumstances you have those who push the envelope, or in some cases outright fraudulently game the system. Over the years of the 8(a) program there were several cases of companies who looked to be minority- or women-owned and operated, but in actuality were fronts for the big boys! Perhaps they were technically owned by a minority but controlled by a non-minority person or persons.

John was very careful to make sure that we three (minority) owners of Red River Shipping actually controlled and ran our company. We had a lot of expert help, but John made it clear from the outset that our company would be run by, and die, survive, or thrive, based on our decisions and operational control.

I want to give a big shout-out to our two partner companies and the outstanding men and women who worked for them and who helped John, JJ, and me tremendously. John's stroke of genius was to structure business relationships with Bill Charrier of American Automar, and Pete Johnson of Pacific Gulf Marine (PGM). American Automar, located in Georgetown, was our partner on the ship ownership side, and PGM, headquartered in New Orleans, was our ship operations partner. Both of these companies were/are outstanding at what they do. John found office space for JJ in Georgetown so that he could have access to American Automar as he ran the ship-ownership side of our business, and I relocated down to New Orleans and shared office space with PGM so that I could take advantage of their day-to-day shipboard operations expertise. Thus, John had assembled his crew.

At this point we were really starting to get our shit (sorry, I mean "ship") together. I could clearly see now how, and why, we were heading for 360° Wealth. We had all six propeller blades working for us.

We were AWARE of what we ultimately wanted. John and I had been on a collision course because we each knew we wanted to own and operate ships, and each of us knew there were missing pieces to our respective puzzles. The key here is that we didn't focus on what we didn't have, we focused on what we wanted. And as simple as it sounds, you can't get what you want if you don't know what you want! Awareness is ALWAYS the first step.

From the outset we NAVIGATED toward our final destination (our outcome). For us, the metaphoric chart that we laid before ourselves was a maze of government Requests For Proposals (RFP's), shipyard contracts, maritime regulations, union negotiations, and nuanced government programs. Again, as simple as it sounds, if you don't know where you're going, ALL charts are useless.

With our chart before us we set a COURSE to arrive at our destination. In the beginning a course always seems daunting, and in the end you realize that it's usually really straight forward. For us, our course was to find foreign-flag ships that had certain operational characteristics, that were for sale within a certain price range, buy the ship, re-flag it and bring it under the U.S. flag, bid on a U.S. government contract (through the Military Sealift Command), win the contract because of our 8(a) Set Aside preference, charter the ship, and make boatloads (pun intended) of money! Simple, right?

As you read this today, you might laugh at what was our INNOVATION propeller blade. But remember, that's what the Innovation blade is all about – a new innovation! Years from now your kids will probably laugh at whatever turned out to be your Innovation blade. One of the key innovations for us at the time we created Red River was the fax machine! It literally was a game changer in regard to increasing and enhancing the speed at which business was done. I'll never forget the first time I saw a fax machine in action. One of our operational partners from American Automar, Bruce Carlton, walked me into the copy room and pointed to a bulky machine that was making a weird whining noise. He said, "The bankers are sending over that contract addendum we discussed earlier." I looked over at the machine and this stream of paper began to spit out from it. In less than five minutes we were back in the conference room looking over a three-page legal document that had been sent to us from Norway! Do you know how long it would have taken for that simple, but crucial, addendum to reach us by regular mail? Yes, the fax machine was indeed a key innovation of that day; and an important blade in the process that propelled us to 360° Wealth.

We were very clear on our OUTCOME. Our specific outcome was to win a U.S. federal government contract, specifically with the Military Sealift Command (MSC). Even more specifically we wanted to find a contract that was "set aside" for a minority-owned business under the 8(a) program, because we felt that was our best shot. So as you can see, we were extremely focused.

And, we were building a CREW. We had partnered with two outstanding companies in American Automar and Pacific Gulf Marine. We intended to make all the decisions and call all the shots per the letter of the 8(a) program, and we had an entire team of expert and experienced advisors at our disposal. They were going to help us find a foreign-flag ship, help us negotiate the financing, advise us on bidding on the set-aside contract, and consult with us on the operation of the vessel. The only piece of our crew that was missing at this point was the captain of our ship.

And at that point all hell broke loose!

19

Captain Of Your Ship & Master Of Your Universe

We marine engineers would like to think that we are the Masters of the Universe aboard ship, if for no other reason than because nothing would run, including the ship itself without the engineers! But that, of course is wishful thinking. After all, they don't call the Captain of a ship "Master" for nothing!

Even though I was an engineer aboard ship for several years, it was my close observation of the Masters on each ship that helped me tremendously when it came to propelling toward my 360° Wealth. Even when I owned my shipping company, there were times when the Captain called the shots. Aboard ship the captain truly is Master and Commander.

Throughout history, a ship's captain has been an almost God-like individual, exercising absolute power over his ship and his crew. From an authority standpoint, not much has changed in modern day seafaring. Even today a ship's Captain still has enormous operational and legal power at his (or her) disposal -- yes, in the last 40 years we have seen women rise to the position of Captain. About time!. A Sea Captain has a tremendous amount of pressure and responsibility. Any Captain will tell you their job is unique in its solitude. It may often be lonely "at the top of the mast" but they'll also tell you their responsibilities to the crew and the owners of the ship are very serious indeed. And the almost dictatorial power one is given to manage these is not to be taken lightly.

Just like as the captain of your wealth voyage you are the ultimate person in charge, so too is the Master or Captain on board a cargo or passenger ship. A Captain is, simply, overall in charge of the entire vessel and the highest authority at sea. More specifically, he or she is in charge of safety of the crew, the vessel, the cargo, and a host of other things. The Captain is also charged with ensuring that all international and local laws are obeyed. Even though a ship is oftentimes considered a sovereign nation in any port, the Captain, crew, and even the vessel still must respect local authorities and laws.

The Captain is responsible for the safe navigation of the ship. They're also responsible for the discipline of the crew.

And, while most commercial ships no longer have jails (or brigs), the Captain does have the right to lock someone up aboard their ship. Even to this day a ship's Captain is judge, jury, and executioner. Well, I don't think a ship's master can actually execute a crewmember in this day and age, but they're still really powerful and their decisions are final.

Sorry engineers, but even though the Chief Engineer is directly responsible for the ship's machinery, the Chief reports to the Captain and the movement of the Engines are under the Master's control.

And, sorry Chief Mate! You may think you are "the man" when it comes to cargo, but the Captain is still overall responsible for the cargo and its stowage. It may sound a little odd, but a ship's Captain has profit and loss (P&L) responsibility for the operation of the ship, too. Nowadays crew wages are direct deposited into their respective bank accounts, but it's the Captain who determines who gets paid what each pay period.

A ship's Captain is responsible for, and must attend to, all the certifications as they pertain to the ship, whether from the country in which the ship is registered, or the Classification Society (like American Bureau of Shipping or Lloyds, etc.) that inspects and certifies the ship.

The Captain also communicates with all the shore authorities in any port in which the ships calls regarding any commercial or other matters, including in response to oil spills or other accidents. Finally, the Captain is responsible for ensuring that proper and accurate records are kept by the vessel and made available to shore authorities in the event of an accident or when otherwise required.

And, since most commercial cargo ships don't carry doctors, if anyone aboard needs medical attention the Captain must ensure that approved adequate supplies are onboard to provide this, or to seek shore medical assistance, including medical evacuation in some cases where it is possible. Every ship's Master must carry a license that is recognized by the country under which the ship is registered. In the United States, the recognizing and certifying body for all ship's officers (Captain, Chief Engineer, all Mates, and Assistant Engineers) is the U.S. Coast Guard.

Just like building your wealth from the ground up, a merchant mariner must sail his or her way to Master; amassing a certain amount of time in each of the lower levels and passing a rigorous exam at each stage.

In many respects, ship owners are very much like corporate investors, in that they're very particular about the people they appoint as Masters, since they entrust millions of dollars of ship and cargo to this one individual.

Owners, like investors, are super sensitive to a Master's ability to get a ship under way and to keep it making way. The financial consequences of a ship not operating, for whatever reason, are disastrous. Merchant (i.e. cargo) ships typically run at a cost of tens of thousands of dollars a day.

So, given the enormity of the job, you can imagine I might have been a little nervous when John, Sr., gave me the responsibility of finding the person who would be the Master of our newly acquired $7 million ship! This person was going to be an extension of each of us as owners, and he or she was ultimately going to be the one who determined the success of our operation.

But John had one other criteria that he insisted upon; and this was the reason all hell broke loose. John insisted that the very first captain of our newly acquired ship be black!

At first this took me totally by surprise. Yes, we were a brand-new company, created and run by three black men. And yes, we were pursuing a federal government contract that was set aside for minority-owned companies, but still, the thought of hiring only a black sea captain NEVER entered my mind!

I grew up in what I would consider a completely color-blind household. Sure, I think all six of us – my parents, my three brothers, and I – were well aware that we were the only black family in an overwhelmingly white, middle- to upper-middle class Northwest Washington, DC neighborhood, but that never, ever, seemed to be an issue for me. My parents were loved and respected by our neighbors, and we kids were just "kids" growing up in Chevy Chase, DC. We had sleepovers and ate dinner at several different houses around the neighborhood -- all the time! And all the other neighborhood kids did the same thing at our house. And of course our house was the "home field", and birthplace, of Fourth Floor Football!

But years later when I think about this -- and the mini shit storm it stirred up with our operating partners and with the maritime union, I can see John Sr.'s perspective. Here was an African-American man who had grown up in the 1930s and '40s and who I'm sure was exposed to way more discrimination than I ever was. And, when you add to that John's legal background and his interest in not only doing what was legally right but also respecting the letter of a law and the law's intent, I'm sure he felt that, given the importance of a captain to a ship's operation, it was only appropriate that a black-owned and operated company have a black captain at the helm. After all, in John's mind, if a minority owned company is being given an opportunity to compete with the stipulation that those minorities actually run the show, then it only made sense to have a minority (in this case, a black) captain.

Well, I was very quickly reminded that the U.S. maritime industry didn't work that way!

Red River's union affiliation for its licensed officers, both deck and engine, was District 2 of the Marine Engineer's Beneficial Association, more commonly known as MEBA District 2, or simply MEBA – D2. I won't go into D2's storied past or tell you how an organization named for marine engineers came to also represent licensed deck officers, but the story reads a lot like the movie *Hoffa*; a major motion picture about the rise and demise of union boss Jimmy Hoffa. The (wise) guys I dealt with at the union were straight out of central casting!

My troubles started when I first announced to my operating partners at PGM what John had asked me to find. My primary contacts (and operating partners) at PGM were Dan Kirby, Executive Vice President; Dan Smith, Port Captain; and Tom Federation, Port Engineer. These were three sharp guys and we all became good friends in addition to business partners. Dan Kirby and Dan Smith both held Masters' licenses and had sailed as captain onboard numerous ships. Tom was a licensed Chief Engineer and had also sailed on many different types of vessels. Dan Kirby and Tom were both graduates of my alma mater, Kings Point. Dan Smith was a graduate of the SUNY Maritime Academy in New York. SUNY (State University of New York) Maritime, also known as Fort Schuyler, was one of the six state maritime academies and was located near Kings Point just across the Long Island Sound.

If you recall our earlier discussion on crews, you'll remember that there are different groups, or teams, that we find ourselves either automatically on, or wanting to become a part of. If you recall, we talked about the importance of understanding what crews are and how they are formed as you look to create and live a 360° Wealth lifestyle. Remember, crews are directly related to how you think about yourself. If you understand the power of a crew from a 360° Wealth perspective you'll begin to realize how best to use this human concept. If you can begin to think of crews as 100% inclusive, never exclusive, you will be well on your way to tremendous wealth. In other words, 360° Wealth crews are never formed or joined simply to keep someone out.

This is a very important concept. Remember my definition of a crew -- a group of two or more people who recognize and celebrate a similarity, and/or have a common belief. This, by definition, means that you could be welcomed into any crew (again oftentimes this happens subconsciously) just by thinking of yourself in a certain way. Because when you think a certain way you project yourself a certain way and this is picked up by the crew.

And finally, I hope you remember the key point about crews ....

It's your ability to move in and out of crews, and think of yourself in different ways, that is key in your ability to create 360° Wealth.

When I first told these three exceptionally smart, very experienced, (white) guys that we needed to approach the union and "demand" (John Sr.'s word) an African-American master for our ship, they looked at me like I had three heads!

I don't think their collective shock at my suggestion (John's demand) was borne out of racism, but rather out of their experience, the typical procedure, and the normal process. As Dan Smith explained to me in his "subtle" New York style (I'm paraphrasing), "You can't just waltz into the union and order up a captain based on what you want him to look like!"

Under normal procedures, a shipping company under union contract has some latitude in selecting its captain, but only from the available union candidates. At the time we were crewing the M/V Advantage (our ship) we had a choice of about five guys – none of whom were black. In fact, at the time, MEBA D-2 didn't have any African-American captains at all. And therein lay John's challenge and his quest.

Being of the mindset, based on my family upbringing, that people were people and the color of their skin didn't matter, it was really hard for me at the time to see John's bigger picture, and his viewpoint. I now know that John's "demand" was not borne out of racism either. It wasn't even born out of some desire for affirmative action. I now know that it was actually the fact that the union had no black captains that was John's real point. He simply wanted us (Red River Shipping) to do our part in leveling the playing field for all.

John Morris was a realist, and he was also an astute businessman. We had a long conversation after I'd been put through the wringer with our partners and the union. I explained the situation, the typical process, and the procedure. He took it all in and gave me what I now see was classic 360° Wealth advice. He said, "Stay the course, never forget our desired outcome, and keep working toward it. We may never get exactly what we want, but if we never 'go for' what we want, we'll never get anything!"

Bolstered by his sage advice, I went back to work seeking to find the best candidate I could to be the master on our recently reflagged ship's maiden voyage. Having spent several years at sea and observing many Captains in action – some great, and some not so great -- I focused on the one thing all the great ones had and the not-so-great ones lacked… a mind!

We ended up selecting an outstanding captain with lots of experience. George had the added benefit of sailing aboard PGM operated ships before and he therefore was familiar with the type of operation we were setting up at Red River. And because I kept "going for it," as John implored me to do, I was able to find among the union ranks a well-qualified African-American Chief Mate. We selected Hugh not simply because he was black but because he was qualified and he was successfully working his way up to become captain. John Sr., John Jr., and I were proud to give him that chance. Hugh, just like George, had that one thing I believed one needed, above all else, to lead and succeed – a working mind!

Yes, to be an effective Captain of your ship and a Master of your universe, it takes one thing above all else. Your ability to think. Your ability to develop thoughts, organize and prioritize those thoughts, and take action on those thoughts is absolutely key to success! In a nutshell, your ability to use that super computer that we all came equipped with is the key to making the Wealth Propeller spin.

Our minds, or brains, are the generators or creators of all our thoughts. And if you don't know it already, your mind is absolutely, off the charts, incredible!

How incredible is your brain?

Did you know a bee has a brain the size of a grain of salt? And yet, it can do many functions your brain can. Bees can communicate between themselves, are aware of magnetic and electric fields, always know the time, and as tiny as their bodies are, can land precisely where they mean to, even on a windy day. All with about one hundred neurons!

Your brain has about one billion neurons, a mere ten million times the size of a bee, so what do you think you're capable of?

Here, check this out. Just think about the simple act of "greeting" or "seeing" someone. It takes you only a few one hundredths of a second to get a visual image of a person. In less than a quarter of a second you take in all that visual information and create a 3-D, full-color image of the person's face, having run that image through your database of thousands of images stored in your memory, and determine if you know this person or if they are someone you have never experienced before. If you have seen this person before, your brain will let you know, even though you may never have seen this face in this particular setting, lighting, or position, or with this particular expression on their face.

In less than a second you will receive detailed information about this person. You will get numerous ideas, associations, and images that are connected with this person. Simultaneously, your brain will also interpret the expression on his or her face and trigger certain emotions and feelings about this person and decide on what course of action you should take, and possibly starting to move certain muscles in response to all this information. Perhaps a message will be sent to your vocal chords to utter certain words like, "Hi, Jane."

Even though this all happens in literally a second, it is in real time and your brain is constantly updating and adjusting to the situation. Your brain will adjust your body position for optimal balance. It will simultaneously monitor the surrounding environment, the sights, sounds, smells, and adjust accordingly, all the while maintaining your physiological systems such as heart rate, body temperature, and emotional response. And so it goes, every second of every day for as long as you live!

Pretty awesome, huh?

If your brain can do this on auto-pilot, think about what it's capable of doing if you direct it in some way. Are you starting to see the possibilities?

20

Great Circle Sailing

You and I started this voyage way back in the 15th century, when almost everyone thought the world was flat. Then this Italian dude, backed by a Spanish couple, hops in a boat and sets sail. He's banking that there is a quicker way to get to the "Promised Land" of his day.

So he heads out of port and takes a right, instead of a left. He's not convinced the earth is flat, so he decides to push the envelope.

Long story short ....

The dude not only doesn't fall off the edge of the supposedly flat earth, but he finds a whole "new world," where the people look different, talk differently, and probably even smell different.

But, this dude -- Columbus is his name, in case you forgot – he's okay with all that "different" stuff because he knows he can convert them to his way of thinking and get them to do his dirty work, and they have a lot of great foods, spices, and gold!

Today we think back on Columbus and wonder how he could have been so naive.

Well, the truth is, he was just a guy with an idea, an inkling, of how the world could be.

And he went for it!

And I'll bet you're glad he did, because today, more than 500 years later, your life is the way it is in large part because guys like Columbus thought there could be another way to see things!

> **This is what mariners do. We set a destination and go for it!**
> **And this is what the 360° Wealthy do! We think about things in a different way, then we propel toward it!**
> **And in each case, the world changes as a result!**

The biggest difference between the 360° Wealthy and the rest of the world is that we take action in a specific way. You see, lots of people think about being rich ….

But the 360° Wealthy, like salty sailors, take specific action.

Things don't always turn out the way we plan, and we often course-correct, but we almost always arrive at our destination.

Back in the 20th century (yeah, way back then!), everyone thought that to be a shipping magnate you had to be old, European, and come from inherited wealth. Then these three American dudes, who looked nothing like Europeans, found a ship originally built by Norwegians, but subsequently owned by Peruvians, and they set sail on a unique entrepreneurial voyage. They're banking there is a quicker way to get to the "Promised Land" of their day. They go about their business in a 360° Wealthy way.

So they head into a corporate board room and take a right, instead of a left. They're not convinced the shipping industry is old, all white, or exclusively non-U.S.; so they push the envelope.

Long story short ....

The dudes not only don't fall flat on their faces, but instead show the whole world that shipping entrepreneurs can look different, talk differently, and even run their company differently.

And these guys are perfectly okay with all that, because they know there's no need to convert anybody to their way of thinking.

How amazing a world we live in where a 25 year old (kid) can dream of a business in a specific industry, with specific types of partners, all of whom create a first of its kind business structure, and have the time of their lives while doing it.

And do you want to know the irony of ironies?

John Morris, Sr., John Morris, Jr., and I created a shipping enterprise with the specific intent to win 8a Set Aside contracts with the Department of Defense's Military Sealift Command (MSC), reflag ships, charter those ships to MSC, and eventually enter the PL 480 (USAID Food for Peace) program and make boat-loads (pun totally intended) of money!

The irony of ironies is that we were NEVER given an 8a Set Aside contract because MSC never created one! Every MSC contract we won, we won in an open and competitive bidding process. Yes, we competed with the Big Boys, and yes, we were competitive!

We also (ironically) never transported a PL480 cargo! It was just never in the cards. And, in the end all turned out just fine – in a 360 wealthy sort of way. Just another example of (a) being able to effectively course-correct, (b) the importance of seeing when a course change is necessary, and (c) figuring out which course to switch to.

Just so we're clear, neither The Call nor the message of this written oratory is about Affirmative Action. Rather it's all about the many components and facets of total (360°) wealth. It's my belief that we "got what we got" because of who we were, not what we happened to look like. And I for one like it a lot better when the world works that way!

Today I think back on those three dudes – one of whom I know rather intimately -- and marvel at the abundance of opportunity in this world. And how so much of life is there for the taking.

You, as a fellow sister/brother wealth seeker might also marvel:

- At how much wealth can be created
- About the relationships you can build, nurture, and enjoy
- At the freedom and creativity you can have
- Or at the value, joy, and usefulness you can bring to the world

So go for it!

And if you're already in the process of going for it, and you're currently on an exploratory voyage to wealth, then keep on keeping on.

Bon Voyage! I'll see you in port!

21

Which Way Does Your Propeller Spin?

Our voyage together is almost over. And before we tell the engine room, "We're finished with engines (FWE)" and record in our log book that the voyage has officially ended, let's take another, closer look at our 360° Wealth propeller.

As we embarked on this 360° Wealth voyage I revealed the blades of our Wealth Propeller in this order:

Awareness

Navigation

Chart Your Course

Team (aka Crew)

Outcomes

Innovations

But if you re-arrange the order of the blades ever so slightly you uncover the real power behind this propulsion system and the seventh piece of the model. Let's have a look and see what our propeller reveals when we order our blades in a different way.

Awareness

Chart Your Course

Team (aka Crew)

Innovation

Outcomes

Navigation

The 7th piece, and the hub of the entire model is ACTION! There really is no "having" without first "doing." So get off your stern (that's the rear end of a ship, by the way), and get into action. 360° Wealth is yours for the taking. But you gotta take it.

I wish you fair winds and following seas!

In eighteen hundred eighty-eight
Our ship sailed the Gibraltar Strait.

We had three partners and a master plan
And many marveled at how smooth the business ran.

We grew by night; we grew by day;
We relied on outside experts to show our way.

A Wealth Propeller also helped us know,
Effortlessly showing us how to find the way to go.

The finest union sailors were employed onboard;
A common and worthy goal they all worked toward.

Decks full of cargo, containers, ropes, and wire
Each man praying the ship would stay on-hire.

For if the battle were not smartly fought
This 360° Wealth seeking voyage would be for naught.

But John, JJ, and Del had a dream,
So they worked together as one hell of a team.

They hoped and dreamed that in wealth they would arrive,
Realizing of course that it takes more than just money to truly
thrive.

In the end it was 360° Wealth upon which they did land,
And compared to monetary wealth this was way way more grand.

So what's the moral of this particular poetic pitch?
It's time to get your ship together and stop just thinking about
getting rich!

Now, go and TAKE SOME ACTION!